F. ERNEST JOHNSON

A VITAL

ENCOUNTER

CHRISTIANITY
and COMMUNISM

Edited by
the Board of Social and Economic Relations
of The Methodist Church and Published by

ABINGDON PRESS  New York • Nashville

A VITAL ENCOUNTER: CHRISTIANITY AND COMMUNISM

Copyright © 1962 by Abingdon Press

Library of Congress Catalog Card Number: 62-11521

SET UP, PRINTED, AND BOUND BY THE
PARTHENON PRESS, AT NASHVILLE,
TENNESSEE, UNITED STATES OF AMERICA

FOREWORD

Several years ago the Board of Social and Economic Relations of The Methodist Church decided that an important area for study by the Christian Church was the challenge of Communism to Christianity. An application for a grant to support such a study was made to the Fund for the Republic and was approved.

This interest of the board follows a long and lively tradition in The Methodist Church stemming from the writings and ministry of John Wesley, its founder, who coupled a strong evangelical witness with activities in the education of children and adults, the establishment of orphanages and homes, interests in health and education, the publication of books, improvement in the lot of prisoners, and concern for the wages and working conditions of miners.

This concern has been sharpened materially in the modern day by the appeal which Communism is making to those who are living in underdeveloped economies or are underprivileged in developed economies. The board's study was described as one that would attempt to define both Communism and Christianity in terms of their philosophical and theological foundations and their expression in economics, political life, and social and international relations. Of particular interest were the contrasts and similarities of the two and the challenge with which each confronts the other ideologically and institutionally.

In attempting to implement these objectives, the board appointed a committee chaired by Dr. John Herr of Philadelphia. This committee has worked diligently on the project, and great appreciation is expressed by the board to its members, Dr. W. Henry Goodloe, Dr. Georgia Harkness, the Rev. Robert C.

Howe, Mrs. E. E. Kinkel, Bishop Donald H. Tippett, and Bishop Lloyd C. Wicke.

The first phase of the project was reflected in the book *Christianity and Communism; an inquiry into relationships,* edited by Merrimon Cuninggim and published by Southern Methodist University Press, Dallas, Texas, 1958. That book resulted from the study by the faculty of the Perkins School of Theology, Southern Methodist University, to discover those areas of concern in the relationship between Christianity and Communism which may call for further research and investigation in successive stages of the study.

The conclusions provided the board by the faculty indicated the direction for phase number two. The faculty advised that future study should be directed toward the sociological, economic, and political confrontation of Christianity and Communism. The world-shaking events since 1958 in which the United States and the Soviet Union have played so great a part clearly validate the wisdom of the faculty.

The board entered upon the second phase of the project by engaging Dr. F. Ernest Johnson of New York City, director for many years of the research department of the Federal Council of Churches, and formerly professor of education at Teachers College, Columbia University, to direct the inquiry. He himself has described the task as follows:

Much has been written about the antagonism between Christianity and Communism; this we take for granted. What we want to learn is how it comes about that people whose beliefs and ideals should be expected to make them hostile to Communism often are attracted to it, perhaps even to the point of affiliation, but at least to the extent of assuming a tolerant or sympathetic attitude. We are particularly interested in the nature of the appeal made by Communism to persons reared in the Christian faith or under the influence of Christianity.

The board engaged a team of highly respected and knowledgeable consultants to work with Dr. Johnson in the project. The members of the team are:

Dr. Paul B. Anderson, Special Agent on Ecumenical Affairs

and Policy of the International Committee of the YMCA

Dr. M. Searle Bates, professor of missions at Union Theological Seminary

Dr. John C. Bennett, dean of the faculty of Union Theological Seminary and the Reinhold Niebuhr Professor of Social Ethics

Dr. George S. Counts, professor emeritus of education, Teachers College, Columbia University

Dr. Charles W. Forman, the James Professor of Missions, and director of graduate studies in religion in the graduate school, Yale Divinity School

Dr. Goodwin Watson, professor of education. Teachers College, Columbia University

Dr. James Alter, Director of Christian Retreat and Study Center, Dehra Dun, UP, India

The inquiry by Dr. Johnson and his team of consultants and a large group of advisors centered on the reasons for the appeal of Communism in sociological, economic, and political terms. Some of the central questions to which the inquiry was addressed are: What is the nature of Communism? What is the basic appeal of Communism? What is the nature of the challenge it presents to the Christian faith and to Western culture particularly related to securing the allegiance of people? What are some of the issues which require decision by persons in the non-Communist orbit and particularly those in the United States?

The board is profoundly grateful to Dr. Johnson, his consultants, and those many others whose names are not listed but whose contributions were invaluable. This volume is commended for study to general readers and especially to the Christian community. It is hoped that it will contribute greatly to the increase of understanding and will eventuate in good and constructive action.

A. Dudley Ward

General Secretary

Board of Social and Economic Relations
The Methodist Church

CONTENTS

I. THE COMMUNIST TIDE 9

II. THE NATURE OF COMMUNISM 28

III. THE APPEALS OF COMMUNISM 52

IV. COMMUNIST METHODS OF
WINNING SUPPORT 78

V. COMMUNISM AND RELIGION 98

VI. SOME ISSUES NEEDING ANALYSIS 127

VII. TOWARD A VALID STRATEGY FOR
MEETING THE COMMUNIST CHALLENGE 150

INDEX 184

1
THE COMMUNIST TIDE

The swift advance of Communism over a large part of
the world since the Russian Bolshevik Revolution in 1917 is one
of the most startling developments since the Christian era began.
A majority of the human race has now either been brought under
Communist rule or been heavily influenced positively or nega-
tively by the challenge of Communism. The word "challenge" is
used advisedly, since it is of the essence of the Communist movement not only to frighten and terrify with its recourse to violence,
but also to stimulate and excite men's minds by the sheer force
of its dynamism. While it enslaves to a terrifying degree those
over whom it establishes control, it also enlists people in absorb-
ing, purposeful activity. These facts give significance to comparative population figures in the Western-oriented nations and in
the Communist bloc: Most startling is the fact that the expansion from control of 200,000,000 to control of nearly a billion
has come in 15 years—since 1944.

To what extent the millions under Communist rule are in
sympathy with the respective Communist regimes is a matter of
perpetual dispute, but the relative stability of Communist governments is stubborn fact. Those who are best informed seem to
have little expectation of a collapse of international Communism in the foreseeable future. There is no longer any warrant
for assuming that the domestic political and economic policy
of the Soviet Union—as distinguished from its foreign policy—
will be reversed, though it will undoubtedly undergo change, as
every historic movement has done. The stability of the Red-
China regime is less evident, but if account is taken of its rela-

tively recent establishment, its strength is no less impressive. One of the best-informed authorities on the subject wrote in 1959, a decade after the Chinese Communists took over the government: "During these ten years Communist China has emerged as one of the most dynamic, disrupting, and disturbing influences on the world scene." [1]

An International Movement

These two great powers have become the major instruments of a revolutionary movement of unprecedented proportions and of novel character. Unlike earlier political power aggregates that have made history, this movement is more than an imperial alliance whose essence is nationalism. It is rightly called international Communism, because its dynamism is ultimately dependent on an appeal that is international in character and scope, utilizing nationalism as a universal drive but transcending nationalism as a political ideal. The spectacle of a Moscow-Peking axis is continually attracting attention by the rifts and rivalries that attend it, but the significant thing about it is the fact that it exists at all. The common concern of those widely separate empires cannot be found in intrinsic "national interest" or in the political configuration of the contemporary world. Rather, the common factor is an idea, a conviction, a vision, a purpose —sufficiently elemental to cut through political and ethnic boundaries. The nature and source of the phenomenal Communist drive we shall be exploring in these pages, in terms of its impact on the ideals and institutions of the Western world, shaped as the latter so largely are by biblical tradition. First, however, we must try to see the picture in broad outline.

The plain fact is that during little more than a generation the political face of the world has changed to a degree that would have been incredible if foretold in my student days before the First World War. The events of the intervening years have brought shock and bewilderment to the Western world—first, by disclosure of the weak foundations of peace and order among the nations; secondly, by the rise of a brutal totalitarianism of

---

[1] A. Doak Barnett, *Communist China and Asia: Challenge to American Policy* (New York: Harper and Brothers, 1960), p. 1.

the right, in fascist and Nazi forms; and thirdly, by a revolutionary totalitarianism of the left which has shaken the foundations of democracy and political morality and has relentlessly attacked all traditional religious faiths and institutions.

If this were the whole truth about international Communism, then of course there would have been no occasion for writing this book, which is not concerned with mere "tide stemming"— usually a futile endeavor. It is concerned, rather, with finding a valid approach to the solution of a major problem of the contemporary world. But serious inquiry must begin with a steady look at facts and an unglossed account of realities.

Purpose and Scope of This Study

As noted in the Foreword to this volume, the study here reported was preceded by an inquiry conducted by a group of scholars who explored the philosophical aspects of the relationship between Christianity and Communism and the concern therewith of theologians and of social and political scientists. The resulting group of essays [2] give an account of Communism as a system of social and political thought and as a way of life. The present volume necessarily deals with philosophical, ideological, and theological questions, but in a setting of social and political situations—with characteristic features of the Communist movement as seen by persons who have studied intensively its manifestations in different parts of the world and as seen by religious leaders who have lived through the encounter between Communism and Christianity in critical situations.

The reader will quickly sense that the title of the book is imprecise in that much of what it records is as relevant to other faiths as to Christianity. This is because of the inclusive character of Communist antagonism to religion. The title seems justified, however, both by the preponderance of Christianity among the religions professed and practiced in many strategic areas where Communism is pressing hard for acceptance, and by the fact that this study is an expression of specifically Christian responsibility

[2] Merrimon Cuninggim, ed., *Christianity and Communism* (Dallas: Southern Methodist University Press, 1958).

for the moral and spiritual outcome of the growing encounter between the spiritual heritage of the Western world and this new self-proclaimed foe of the religious heritage that informs our Western culture.

It should be stressed, however, that we are not here concerned primarily or specifically with the Christian "mission" to Communists, although attention will be given to the "person-to-person" aspect of the encounter that is being studied. Rather, our major concern throughout will be with the total encounter and what is indicated as a sound and viable strategy vis-à-vis Communism to which Christians as citizens can, consistently with the Christian ethic, give support. It cannot be said too emphatically that the Christian Church has no corporate political or economic position to defend as far as specific measures and policies are concerned. The more church membership increases the more remote is the likelihood of achieving consensus on political and social issues. It follows that such a study as is here reported must deal with analysis more than with prescription, must present tentative judgments rather than dogmatic conclusions.

I have been wisely cautioned against ambiguity in the use of the collective term "we." When it occurs in the text does it mean we Christians, we Americans, we of the West, or we who are engaged in this study? Since the ambiguity is partly inherent in the use of language, chief reliance must be placed on the context, in the light of what has been said above, for the nature of the discussion makes it inevitable that the connotation will not be strictly uniform. Perhaps it is substantially accurate to say that in general what is meant is "we" as Americans, inheritors of the Western tradition, and giving allegiance to the Judaeo-Christian ethic.

A Continually Changing Scene

The task of preparing this volume has been augmented because it synchronized with sudden changes in Communist strategy and tactics and an intensification of the challenge of Communism to the Western world. Manifestly, the undertaking involves the risk of introducing matters that may be less relevant when these words

12

are in print than they seem today. What is more, events will almost surely occur in the interim whose absence from the present scene may conspicuously "date" portions of what will be found in these pages.

There is another side to the matter, however. We are studying a revolutionary movement that has deep historical roots, and the key to an understanding of revolution is furnished more by history than by reference to the sequence of contemporary events. Moreover, in spite of the frustrating unpredictability of such events, political and cultural, it is in a time like ours that the elemental, the universal, in human nature, which furnishes the best key to history, is thrown into sharpest relief. Although we are quite unable to forecast specific developments, we can see, as we could not in normal times, why some events we took for granted can no longer be expected to happen. These are days of disillusionment for all who have carried over facile assumptions of the nineteenth century. This applies to Christians who looked for a golden age just over the hill; it applies also to American patriots who saw their country marching steadily on toward its "manifest destiny" and a "brave new world." In no small part the equipment for living in a revolutionary age consists in relinquishing, or in rendering tentative, customary assumptions and in attainment of a more trustworthy perspective on human affairs. We have to be acclimated to change—ready for alternative eventualities. All this takes time; it cannot be accomplished in the intervals between summit conferences or diplomatic "incidents." The stubborn realities that have to be faced may be feebly expressed or little affected by new headlines in the daily press.

To be sure, this generalization implies the assumption—a fairly large one, many people fear—that we are *not* on the verge of total destruction, East and West alike. Indeed, it is one of the ironies of history that what not long ago seemed to be an inevitable and impending Armageddon appears to have been averted, for the present at least, by the mere contemplation of the immeasurable and indiscriminate destruction with which it would flood the world. We must hope and pray that "for the present" means long enough to establish a viable world order. What we shall be concerned with in this book, therefore, it is reasonable to expect, will be relevant to the world situation no matter what vicissitudes await us in the immediate future.

Yet a caveat is surely in order here. The theory of "nuclear stalemate" as an effectual deterrent from resort to general war seems to have lost some of its force—as of summer, 1961. This is due less to the "trigger-finger" notion of the sudden precipitation of unintended war—a patently real danger—than to the current hardening of attitudes and stiffening of policies as a result of such crucial developments as the "Berlin crisis" and the lamented abortive attempt at invasion of Castro's island fortress in the Caribbean Sea. It would seem that in the United States there is a marked trend toward an ultimatum, a no-matter-what policy in dealing with the Soviet Union. Regardless of developments in the immediate future, this tendency toward a policy of calculated risk, which involves setting limits to negotiation and taking a chance on nuclear war, confronts us all with an ethical issue that belongs in the "ultimate" category. We shall return to this question. It seems appropriate here, however, to suggest that the issue—like so many basic ethical issues—is clouded by the inherent uncertainty of events and resists all attempts to make it "clear-cut." Many persons who call for a showdown with the Kremlin or with Castro's revolutionary regime in Cuba are doubtless counting confidently on "calling a bluff" and not consciously gambling on victory in a major war. Others seem to be saying, in effect, that some issues justify the risk of war, however great, and the risk of consequences, however dire and far-reaching.

"East and West"

A troublesome question of terminology arises, in writing on Communism, over the use of the terms East and West, Eastern and Western, to designate the Communist and non-Communist spheres, respectively. That the usage is imprecise is patent when one thinks of India, and even of the present map of Western Europe. However, three considerations favor retaining these imprecise terms. (1) They are in general use in this context by even the most discriminating writers. (2) No alternative presents itself that does not involve awkward and repetitive language. (3) More fundamentally, profound students of political and cultural history find a conspicuous contrast between Russian history and that of Western Europe. Said the historian Hans Kohn:

> Since the end of antiquity, Europe has been divided into East and West: Constantinople and Rome, the Eastern and Western Empires, Greek Orthodox and Roman Catholic Christianity. After the fall of Constantinople to the Turks, at the close of the Middle Ages, Russia emerged as the most powerful representative of the East. In the West, with the development of the parliamentary system and the beginnings of the industrial revolution, England became, more than geographically, the typically Western country.[3]

He refers to Russia as the first non-Western society to come under the impact of modern Western civilization. The cultural and political separateness of Russia from the West is a theme that informs the work of some of her greatest writers. These considerations have governed the use of these disputed terms in this book.

The New "Communist Manifesto"

In order to present a factual picture of the present strength of the Communist movement that would be as accurate as possible, the finalizing of this first chapter was deferred until most of the analysis presented in the later chapters had been completed. It so happens that as this is being written there comes to hand an extraordinary document promulgated by the Central Committee of the Communist Party of the Soviet Union. It contains the "program" of the party presented to its twenty-second congress in October, 1961. By the time these lines appear in print the program will presumably have been formally

[3] Kohn, ed., *The Mind of Modern Russia* (New Brunswick, N.J.: Rutgers University Press, 1955), p. 3. Used by permission.

adopted. In any case, it may be taken as present Communist doctrine in the Soviet Union. The document is being referred to as another "Communist Manifesto." It is long, verbose, and repetitive, but some portions of it may well be noted here as indicating the ways in which the Soviet Union—chief repository of Communist leadership—is presently seeking to promote international Communism on a global scale.

It is pointed out that the objectives of the Communist party of the U.S.S.R. are two: (1) The transformation of capitalism into socialism; and (2) the building of Communism on a world scale. The socialist principle—"From each according to his abilities, to each according to his work"—the party claims now to have implemented in the U.S.S.R. It "insures that the members of society have a material interest in the fruits of their labor; it makes it possible to harmonize personal and social interests in the most effective way and serves as a powerful stimulus for increasing productivity of labor, developing the economy and raising the people's standard of living." [4] The supreme Communist goal is again declared to be: "From each according to his ability, to each according to his needs."

Significantly, the new program includes the statement: "In the coming twenty years payment according to one's work will remain the principal source for satisfying the material and cultural needs of the working people." This bald statement suggests confidence that the Russian people are ready to accept it because they are "sold" on the glowing picture of the remoter future in the midst of which it appears. Yet the party by no means rests its case on social theory. A most significant aspect of the program is its emphasis on education. With all power in its hands it stands apart from and over the people and strives to mold the people according to its desired patterns. As *Pravda* stated unequivocally in a long editorial on July 6, 1956: "As for our country, the Communist party has been, is, and will be the sole master of the minds, the voice of the thoughts and hopes, the leader and organizer of the people in their entire struggle for Communism."

[4] "Text of the Soviet Party's Draft Program," New York *Times* (August 1, 1961). Used by permission.

Borrowing a term from the theological vocabulary, one might say that the current Soviet program embodies "realized eschatology" on a secular scale; the ideal society is continually spoken of as achieved by Communism, yet the program bristles with tasks still to be done.

War Not Inevitable

Of special importance is the new declaration concerning the possibility of avoiding war. The Soviet party "maintains that forces capable of preserving and promoting world peace have arisen and are growing in the world. It is becoming possible to establish essentially new relations between states." [5] This statement is later significantly elaborated:

It is possible to avert a world war by the combined efforts of the mighty Socialist camp, the peace-loving non-Socialist countries, the international working class and all the forces championing peace. The growing superiority of the Socialist forces over the forces of imperialism, of the forces of peace over those of war, will make it actually possible to banish world war from the life of society even before the complete victory of socialism on earth, with capitalism surviving in a part of the world. The victory of socialism throughout the world will do away completely with the social and national causes of all wars. To abolish war and establish everlasting peace on earth is a historical mission of Communism. [6]

What may perhaps be regarded as a clarifying commentary on a controversial Communist issue is this paragraph:

Peaceful coexistence serves as a basis for the peaceful competition between socialism and capitalism on an international scale and constitutes a specific form of class struggle between them. As they consistently pursue the policy of peaceful coexistence, the Socialist countries are steadily strengthening the positions of the world Socialist system in its competition with capitalism. Peaceful coexistence affords more favorable opportunities for the struggle of the working class in the capitalist countries and facilitates the struggle of the peoples of the colonial and dependent countries for their liberation. [7]

[5] *Ibid.*
[6] *Ibid.*
[7] *Ibid.*

This seems to mean that it is gratuitous to regard peaceful coexistence—a Leninist formula—as a mere propaganda trick; that it is not "carrot" but "stick," albeit a means of escaping destruction of both East and West. We shall attempt, as our analysis proceeds in subsequent chapters, to find clues to the significance of Communist slogans, declarations, and predictions that abound in ambiguities and apparent contradictions, which this recent manifesto so amply illustrates. It is to be feared that most of us are so much preoccupied with Communist duplicity, deception, distortion, and rationalization that we fail to discern the substance of the Communist appeal as appraised in many parts of the world. Exposure of fallacy and fraud is abundantly justified but is often singularly devoid of effectiveness. In part, we should be humble enough to admit, this may be accounted for by the fact that our own government has, on occasion, played a disingenuous role in international affairs. This is no doubt less a specific allegation than a characterization of diplomatic relationships in general. It is surely important, however, to recognize that as long as diplomacy is an instrument of cold war—as in the lamentable Cuban affair in 1961—official government propaganda can be only an uncertain asset. If there is truth and valid warning in the often-heard lament "We are losing the Cold War," it is in no small part due to the gap between national interest as officially understood, and the code of honor represented by international law—rudimentary as it is—and by the Charter of the United Nations.

Communist Party Strength Today

It is important, when undertaking such an inquiry as we are attempting, to look at the geographic picture and take the measure, so to speak, of the Communist movement on a global scale. Fortunately a recent survey of the status and relative strength of Communist parties throughout the world is available —one that is factual, objective, and official—issued by our State Department as of January, 1961.[8] Major items of this survey are

[8] *World Strength of the Communist Party Organization*, Intelligence Report No. 4489-R-13, Bureau of Intelligence and Research, Department of State, Washington, D. C. January, 1961.

sketched below. The reader is urged to make mental note, for subsequent consideration, of the surprising number of instances of weak and seemingly ineffectual Communist parties which do not at all suggest the "Communist tide" that is causing so much concern. This fact has its own significance and importance.

Europe

Let us first look at the highlights of the State Department's survey.

In the United Kingdom the estimated membership of the party is only 27,000. The party has had no seats in Parliament during the past decade. Membership, at least until recently, has been going down.

In Ireland Communist party membership is negligible.

In the Netherlands the Communist party has but three seats, and party membership is estimated at 12,000. Communist strength seems to have been declining.

In Belgium the party has but two seats, and membership is estimated at 11,000. This is the lowest point since 1929.

France presents a somewhat different picture. Party membership is estimated at 250,000, and the party has ten seats. It polled nearly 4,000,000 votes in the last election. But its strength greatly diminished in the 1958 elections after it had been for twelve years the largest single political party.

The Italian Communist party also attained a position of considerable strength. It has 141 seats and a membership estimated at 1,500,000. The party has a following in almost every social class and geographical area. (Communists control Italy's largest trade union, the CGIL.) It has been losing ground in urban centers but gaining in the underdeveloped south. It is a force to be reckoned with. The significance of Communist strength in predominantly Catholic Italy will be considered later.

Northern Europe might perhaps not inaccurately be called a bulwark against Communism. In Denmark the party has not been able to win any seats and polled about 27,345 votes. The membership is estimated at only 5,000. Communist strength has continually declined in recent years. In Norway Communism has relatively little strength.

In Sweden Communist strength has been appreciable, but in 1958 the party was reported to have made the poorest showing since the war. The Hungarian affair was apparently influential in weakening it. There has been some gain since, however.

Finland's party has fifty seats and over 450,000 votes, but membership is estimated at only 30,000 to 35,000. Communist influence is reported strongest in Lapland, the underdeveloped northernmost province. For historical reasons, however, if for no other, the Finnish people seem to have a mind-set against *Russian* Communism.

The Communist bloc of nations in Europe is, of course, composed of regimented populations in which sentiment and political susceptibility cannot be measured. In Hungary, however, the 1956 revolt apparently shattered the party temporarily. To all intents the power of Communism is absolute in the countries behind the curtain.

South Africa

Paradoxically, the African nations, which have been responsive —sometimes eagerly—to Soviet propaganda have, in general, no great organized Communist strength. This is a striking illustration of the political assets international Communism can find without regard to organized national parties.

Near East

In the Near East Communist parties are, in general, illegal, and Communism is not a strong political force. In Iraq, however, illegal status has not prevented very marked growth of front groups and Communist-led labor unions.

South Asia

Turning to South Asia we find in India a relatively strong Communist party with a polling strength of nearly 12,000,000 votes, holding twenty-nine seats, and with a membership estimated at 230,000. The party itself is apparently quite subservient to Moscow, though the national government is an outstanding example of a democratic socialist regime. The main Communist strength is in organized labor. The party has found peasant support difficult to win, and its strength among students and intellectuals appears to have declined since 1959. The Indian Communist party supported Red China on the Tibetan issue, which appears to have weakened it. Dissolution by the national government of the Kerala regime in 1959, ending twenty-eight months of Communist rule, damaged the party's prestige, which was further weakened by its neutral stand on the Sino-Indian border dispute.

Afghanistan should be noted as a type of small nation that is politically realistic, accepting aid in substantial amounts from the Soviet Union, but avoiding alignment.

In Indonesia an exceptionally well-informed correspondent wrote that there were in 1959 at least three Christians and possibly five who had won seats in parliament on the Communist ticket.

In the Far East we find for the most part either out-and-out Communist regimes, as in North Korea, North Vietnam, and mainland China itself, or neutral regimes, more or less vulnerable to Communist influence.

Latin America

We come now to Latin America, where, with the exception of Cuba, the organized strength of Communism is not great. The other nineteen states have had Communist-inspired episodes and revolutionary disturbances, but Communist ideology and discipline do not, it appears, readily take root in Latin America. The term "outlawed" or its equivalent occurs again and again in the State Department's survey of the political status of Communism. Where legal status has been maintained by Communist parties, or restored to them, their strength in terms of direct political action is meager. Even in Venezuela, Argentina, and Brazil, where party membership is substantial, there is little evidence of Communist political power. Parliamentary representation of Communist parties is inconsiderable.

Cuba, of course, holds a unique position as a new center of Communist social dynamism—no matter how its technical relationship with the Soviet Union is construed. The situation is at present unstable, of course, and the fate of the Castro regime is problematic, if only for economic reasons. The case of Cuba is instructive, for without any evident prior ideological intention it appears to have become a Soviet satellite—physically remote, but definitely in orbit.

Internal and External Threats

My chief purpose in citing data from the State Department's survey has been to point up the disparity between the internal threat of Communism—its disruptive influence within a country —and the fear so widely felt by the Western nations of international Communism. The most striking illustration is, of course, furnished by the United States, where a great reduction in Communist influence in political and civil life has taken place in a relatively short time. Only a few years ago Communist influence in the American labor movement and in various intellectual circles was a matter of common knowledge. It was, to be sure, far from dominant, save in a limited number of organizations. The often repeated charge that our churches had been extensively infiltrated is now recognized as a canard. Anti-Communist hysteria has been widespread, often fostered by political interest and ambition. There can hardly be any question, however, that Communist influence in the United States, especially through front organizations, once attained proportions by comparison with which the contemporary domestic Communist threat is very small.

Important inferences are to be drawn from these facts, but not hastily. In the first place, one evident cause of a waning of Communist strength within non-Communist countries is the sharply restrictive measures that have been taken by governments against Communist activity, notably the banning of Communist parties. Whatever may be the unwholesome effect of forcing a movement underground, when such a policy is implemented by so skillful and energetic an agency as the American FBI, its restrictive effect in quantitative terms can hardly be exaggerated.

At this point, however, it might be instructive to take a look at the world through the eyes of Moscow. In the issue of *Pravda* for January 7, 1961, appears a large front-page editorial entitled "The Unity and Solidarity of the Communists of the Entire World." According to this editorial: "Communist Parties now live and struggle in 87 countries and unite more than 36 million members. During the last three years 12 Communist Parties have sprung up and into the ranks of the international army of Communists three million new active warriors have entered. The Communists lead hundreds of millions of toilers." A few years ago a leading Soviet educator reported the world situation in these words:

The mighty ideas born of the great October Revolution are winning triumphantly the minds and the hearts of millions of people. Marching with the one billion population of the socialist countries are approximately seven hundred million people in former colonial countries which have achieved their independence and six hundred million in lands now struggling for independence. There remain in the countries of the camp of imperialism only about four hundred million. Today, as picturesquely expressed by Mao Tse Tung, "It is no longer the West wind that directs the East wind, but the East wind that directs the West wind."

The Matter of Legal Status

The State Department, in classifying nations with respect to the legal status of Communist parties, has included the United States among the governments that have not made such parties illegal. However, Communism has long been stigmatized in the United States as a subversive movement. The Supreme Court in upholding in June, 1961, the "membership clause" of the Smith Act of 1940 merely put the final authoritative seal upon a policy which had been formulated by Congress and supported in apparently increasing measure by public opinion. The portion of the Smith Act relevant here is the following:

Whoever organizes or helps or attempts to organize any society, group, or assembly of persons who teach, advocate, or encourage the overthrow or destruction of any such government by force or violence; *or becomes or is a member of,* or affiliates with, *any such society, group, or assembly of persons, knowing the purposes thereof—*

Shall be fined not more than $20,000 or imprisoned not more than twenty years, or both, and shall be ineligible for employment by the United States or any department or agency thereof, for the five years next following his conviction.

The ruling and the dissenting opinions in this case raise issues of national policy that need to be weighed, but the important point to emphasize here is that an American policy has been established and judicially confirmed that makes the United States relatively immune internally to the political impact of Communism to which many other nations are exposed. Indeed the fact that Communism in the United States is stigmatized by law and custom greatly increases the difficulty of understanding how it looks to the citizens of countries where it is not underground. A major purpose of this study has been to help American readers to see the face that Communism wears in countries where it has the status of a bona fide political party to which no general opprobrium attaches, for it is not as an underground movement that Communism is challenging the world, but as a highly visible and well advertised enterprise. Subversion by undercover Communist agents is, to be sure, a serious problem for democratic governments, but it is far from comparable to the impact of a movement which, operating in the open and by all effective means, wins over person after person, group after group, and government after government. The fact should be noted, however, that in so far as governments are concerned, except in the case of Kerala, Communism has never achieved power through the freely expressed will of the people.

Moreover, it would be a serious error to equate illegality of status or negligible party membership with ineffectuality. Criticism of legislation or of private attitudes and practices inspired by obsessive fears of Communist intrigue and sabotage is, I believe, very much in order. The violence done to civil liberty by

ill-conceived anti-Communist activities probably often far out-
weighs any valid ends achieved in this way. At the same time, the
mere fact that Communists and the Communist party in a given
country are judged weak or are without legal recognition does
not mean that they are without significance—that they play no
role in the activities of international Communism.

A report received from Argentina during the course of the
present study is illuminating in this connection. Although only
the Communist party and the Communist Youth Federation are
designated as officially accepted agencies of the movement, a dozen
other Communist-led organizations are listed as promoting it,
most of which have headquarters in the European Communist
area. A number of additional agencies infiltrated by Communists
are carrying on propaganda in labor unions and among professional groups. The Communist party publishes many magazines
and a number of newspapers.

Obviously this kind of activity in countries that are, on the
whole, non-Communist and perhaps officially anti-Communist
constitutes planned preparation for the carrying out of Communist designs. Ideology is subordinated to practical concerns of
the people as a whole. It may even be advantageous from the
Communist point of view to avoid issues with patent international implications and to concentrate on here-and-now interests
and needs. The overthrow of the government is probably the last
thing the Communists are concerned about in most countries
where they are active. The over-all aim of Communist propaganda today is to focus attention on human needs and alleged
injustice and exploitation and to prepare the minds of men for
acceptance of the idea that only international Communism has
the answers. It must be said, therefore, that to write, as a well-
known newspaper correspondent did in 1960, that "Communism
has almost ceased to exist as a potent political force in the West"
is only partially true. The statement calls attention, commenda-
bly, to the folly of hysterical anti-Communist crusading, especially in the United States, but it overlooks the indubitable effectiveness of even small-scale Communist propaganda which brings
to light neglected human sufferings and grievances. "Interven-

tion" and "indirect aggression," of which complaint is so widely heard, no matter how reprehensible they may be, result in the first instance from internal grievances. Yet the exploitation of such grievances by international Communism is a global threat.

Since we in the United States have a high-priority responsibility for the future of the Americas it is appropriate here to emphasize conditions that give concern to statesmen in the countries that are our southern neighbors.

It has been well said that the "revolutionary potential" in Latin American countries stems from "a combination of social protest, inadequate economies, and chaotic politics." Who can deny that the United States has contributed to all three? In any case the report made in 1960 to the Organization of American States by the Inter-American Peace Committee was grievously challenging. One passage reads:

> The American community is faced today with a serious crisis which, although not limited to the Caribbean area, is more clearly revealed there than elsewhere.
>
> Underlying this crisis is the striving of the peoples of America to improve their economic and social conditions of life. They aspire to obtain for themselves and for future generations better homes, education, health, and economic security. They wish to do this within a system compatible with the respect for human rights and the effective exercise of representative democracy.

How anyone can read that and still speak contemptuously of foreign aid is something to cavil at. Adlai Stevenson has put the matter tersely: "Communism per se, I am convinced, is not naturally attractive to the bulk of Latin Americans, not even to the many intellectuals who seem most inclined toward it. It is, nevertheless, a magnet that attracts and will continue to draw unhappy people as long as the spokesmen of other political philosophies seem capable only of talk, and can point to no action to right wrongs." [9]

[9] "Red Shadows Over Latin America," The New York *Times Magazine* (August 6, 1961), p. 11.

The Essence of the Matter

What, then, is the real portent of the "Communist tide"? The Soviet Union has become an unprecedented aggregation of political and military power, embracing a score of "nations" and dominating Poland, East Germany, Hungary, Czechoslovakia, Rumania, Albania, Bulgaria, Outer Mongolia, and North Korea, and is allied with a politically reborn China, the most populous country on earth, in a determined effort to make Communism prevail throughout the world. Partly by brutal military might, partly by shrewd diplomacy, partly by an awe-inspiring dynamism, but in no small measure by making itself the ostensible champion of the underprivileged peoples of the earth, this colossus is bent on obliterating the traditions, institutions, and faith of the Western world. Borrowing a well-known question of Lenin's, we are asking "What is to be done?"

2
THE NATURE OF COMMUNISM

Communism is not a new word, nor was it a word of opprobrium until a few decades ago. It is related, obviously, to "community," which, as the philosopher Josiah Royce long ago pointed out, is a concept characteristic of Christianity. The community concept is also a key to modern developments in social theory and in education. The distinctive feature of Communism in the general and original sense of the word, which has been the organizing principle of many community experiments since the one recorded in the book of Acts, is the common ownership of property by a group of people living in close relationship. It has no necessary resemblance to Marxism in any form and is a far cry from the totalitarian political system that we know as Communism today. The rise of this latter phenomenon, which is perhaps more appropriately called Bolshevism, is bound up with the recent history of Russia.

Soviet Russia, heart-land of the international Communist movement, is a political and cultural entity upon which have converged many lines of historical development. To most Americans the very name Russia now denotes first and last the stronghold of a giant conspiracy against the Free World. So to characterize it, however, is to contribute little to an understanding of Communism or of the realities of international politics.

This is not to suggest that the word conspiracy in this context is inaccurate or inappropriate. The foreign policy of the Soviet Union has a conspiratorial aspect, as was made painfully clear at the October, 1960, session of the United Nations General Assembly when a campaign was launched to cripple the UN as at present organized. This, however, as has already been suggested, is indicative chiefly of the fact that the paramount Communist power conceives itself as permanently at war—either cold or hot —with the non-Communist world; it indicates little concerning the nature, the disposition, or the potentialities of the Russian people or of the citizens of any other Communist nation. My "posture" will be that of one concerned less with indictment or apology than with interpretation, motivated by the hope that the agonizing struggle now going on is in the nature of travail— prelude to a new birth.

The West is grievously lacking in background information about Russia, without which the meaning of the present era is elusive. It would be a mistake, of course, to regard Russian history since 1917 as merely an extrapolation of the history of the Russian Empire. The Russian Revolution presents significant aspects of novelty; yet it is not a mutation—if one may use a biological concept in this connection. The degree of continuity, especially in cultural terms, is strikingly large. Because the Communist avalanche has left so many of us in a sort of "now-I've-seen-everything" mood a major concern of one who attempts to write about it must be to place this phenomenon in historical perspective. Perhaps historians who address themselves to the Communist movement in China will find a similar nexus between eras of Chinese history that on the surface seem irreconcilable. The dynamism of the Communist movement in China was strikingly characterized by one of our correspondents, who wrote: "Those who have known China fairly well have been surprised, indeed shocked, by the break which Chinese Communism is making with the past. The repudiation of parental control and even betrayal of parents; the public denunciation of one's best friends; and the submission we have seen to Party loyalty—these are all reversals of Chinese behavior which few of us expected to see."

It has been contended that the American Communist movement should be viewed against the background of certain chapters of American history, as well as that of the Russian Revolution. Many explosive events are recorded by historians, but there is always a continuity to apprehend which is a prime requisite of statesmanship. It is also an essential of Christian ethics, since only in the perspective of history can men understand and cope with the less attractive aspects of collective human behavior.

A Revolutionary "Catechism"

It is highly relevant here, therefore, to point out that Russian Communism did not invent its uncompromising militancy, but found a pattern for its revolutionary strategy already made by the nihilist movement which had grown up largely as a reaction to the autocratic regime of the Tsars. The most striking documentation of this observation is in the "Catechism of a Revolutionist" formulated probably by Nechaev (1847-1882), a younger contemporary of Mikhail Bakunin. The nihilism that flourished in the latter part of the nineteenth century furnished a rationale and a blueprint for the negative, destructive aspect of revolutionary socialism, which served the purposes of the Bolsheviks. Significant portions of the "catechism" are reproduced below.

The revolutionist is a doomed man. . . . Everything in him is absorbed by one exclusive interest, one thought, one passion—the revolution. . . .

[The revolutionist] has broken every connection with the social order and with the whole educated world, with all the laws, appearances and generally accepted conventions and moralities of that world which he considers his ruthless foe. Should he continue to live in it, it will be solely for the purpose of destroying it the more surely. . . .

He knows only one science, the science of destruction. . . .

He despises public opinion. He despises and hates the present day code of morals with all its motivations and manifestations. To him whatever aids the triumph of the revolution is ethical; all that which hinders it is unethical and criminal. . . .

He must be ready to die at any moment. He must train himself to stand torture.

Rigorous towards himself, he must also be severe towards others. All tender, softening sentiments of kinship, friendship, love, gratitude, and even honor itself must be snuffed out in him by the one cold passion of the revolutionary cause. . . .

Each comrade must have at hand several revolutionists of the second and third degree, *i.e.* such as are not entirely initiated. He must consider them as part of the common revolutionary capital placed at his disposal. He must spend his portion of the capital economically, always striving to extract the greatest possible use from it. He is to consider himself as capital, fated to be spent for the triumph of the revolutionary cause; however, he has no right personally and alone to dispose of that capital without the consent of the aggregate of the fully initiated.

When a comrade comes to grief, in deciding the question whether or not to save him, the revolutionist must take into consideration not his personal feelings, but solely the interests of the revolutionary cause. . . .

The admission into the organization of a new member, who has proven himself not in words but in deeds, can be effected only by unanimous agreement.

The revolutionist enters the world of the State and of the educated privileged classes and lives in it only for the purpose of its fullest and quickest destruction. . . . All the worse for him if he has any relations of kinship, friendship or love; he is not a revolutionist if they can stop his hand.

For the purpose of ruthless destruction, the revolutionist may and frequently must live in society, pretending to be something entirely different from what he is. . . .

The Association has no aim other than the complete liberation and happiness of the masses, *i.e.* of the people who live by manual labor. But, convinced that this liberation and the achievement of this happiness is possible only through an all-destroying popular revolution, the Association will by all its means and all its power further the development and extension of those evils and those calamities which must at last exhaust the patience of the people and drive them to a general uprising.

By Revolution the Association does not understand a regulated movement after the classical Western model—a movement which, always bowing to the property rights and the traditions of the social systems of so-called civilization and morality, has until now limited itself everywhere to the overthrow of one political form in order to replace it by another and striven to create a so-called revolutionary state. Only that revolution will be beneficial to the people which will destroy at the very root every vestige of statehood and will annihilate all of Russia's state traditions, institutions and classes.

The Association therefore does not intend to foist on the people any organization from above. The future organization will no doubt evolve out of the popular movement and out of life itself. But this is the business of future generations. Our business is destruction, terrible, complete, universal, and merciless. . . .

To consolidate this world into one invincible, all-destroying force is the sole object of our organization; this is our conspiracy, our task.[1]

I have quoted extensively from this crude and brutal revolutionary document in order to make the Bolshevik era more comprehensible. Perhaps the latter part of Psalm 137 was preserved in the Old Testament canon because of a like concern for historical realism, though its language of hot vengeance is quite as terrible: "O daughter of Babylon, who art to be destroyed; happy shall he be, that rewardeth thee as thou hast served us. Happy shall he be, that taketh and dasheth thy little ones against the stones." (Vss. 8-9.)

Historical Background

Probably no recent writer has contributed more to an understanding of the Russian mind than the historian Hans Kohn. He has even suggested that in the early nineteenth century an affinity —in quality, though not in form—was observable between the notoriously autocratic government of Russia and her revolutionary socialism: That the latter was an inversion of the former. He quotes Bakunin, who in 1870, the very year of Lenin's birth, was predicting the rise of a party

strong by its discipline, by the devotion and passionate self-denial of its members and by its passive obedience to all the orders of a central committee . . . in which it is not the individual who thinks, desires, and acts, but the collectivity. A serious member will understand that only such a discipline can create a collective revolutionary force which, supported by the elemental force of the people, will be able to overthrow the formidable strength of the state.[2]

Kohn also cites the testimony of Thomas Masaryk, who was a close student of Russian history. In 1921 Masaryk said:

---

[1] As quoted in Max Nomad, *Apostles of Revolution* (Boston: Little, Brown and Company, 1939), pp. 228 ff. Used by permission of the author.

[2] *Op. cit.,* p. 31. Used by permission.

The Bolsheviks have accepted Marxism and pride themselves on being its only orthodox adherents. They do not realize how much they owe to Bakunin [1814-1876], the adversary of Marx. From him they took over their mystic faith in the revolution, in the Russian people, in its unique socialist and Communist ability. . . . All the shortcomings which characterized the Russian state, the Russian school, the Russian church, and so on, characterize also the Bolshevik state and regime because they have come from the same people and have undergone the same formation.[3]

The constructive aspect of the Russian communal ethos is impressively characterized by Bernard Pares, who stands high among authoritative interpreters of Russian life and history. He remarks that, in a broad sense, "the past life of Russia was full enough of the instinct of Communism." Continuing, he says:

The village community had to be Communist in its long unequal battle with poor soil and climate. The village holding was held in common by all, with periodical redivisions according to the number of workers, and the villagers would vote on every act of the farmer's year. The whole trend of Russian orthodoxy is to visualize a great community in which all are equal: its favourite word *sobornost*—"cathedralness" if you like—means union in reverence, in the instinct of the community; and at moments of national danger and distress this sense has always swept everyone in Russia into the community; never have I seen this better in its full beauty than at Easter in the Russian front line in 1915, when, incidentally, it was a Marxist who organised and led the church choir.[4]

A strange amalgam, this pre-Leninist Russian ethos! Material-ism, says Kohn, was given by the nihilist a kind of "dogmatic theological setting," making of it a faith. Materialism, messianism, eschatological outlook, idealization of collectivity—this combination was conducive to the growth of totalitarian dictatorship, for totalitarianism is precisely the denial of cultural autonomy and the complete regimentation of the culture by the state in pursuit of predetermined political ends. Science, philosophy, the arts,

[3] *Ibid.*
[4] *Russia* (Baltimore: Penguin Books, Inc. 1943), p. 23. Used by permission of Alfred A. Knopf, Inc.

religion, and the entire value system are pressed, as far as the state finds it possible, into an all-inclusive mold. The scheme has a terrifying meretricious splendor because of its secular apocalyptic vision—a transcendant purpose whose implementation awaited a triumphant messianic Russian nationalism. Did not Dostoevski himself regard the Russian nation as "God-bearing" and entertain the Slavophile vision of a perfect society? Says Kohn: "In the eyes of the Slavophils and in the eyes of the 'progressive' Russian youth alike, Russia was destined to become the model 'socialist' country, in which the social problem would be solved." [5]

In this vision the traditional religion was implicitly and explicitly involved. Russia was Orthodox Russia, and Moscow was thought of as "a Third Rome and the center of world salvation." Yet in the background of that vision of glory was a dark pessimism concerning the capacity of human beings to achieve and maintain freedom in the liberal, individual sense. Berdyaev wrote in 1937:

> The greatest paradox in Russian life and the Russian revolution lies in this, that liberal ideas, ideas of rights as well as of social reform, appeared in Russia to be utopian. Bolshevism showed itself to be much more faithful to certain primordial Russian traditions, to the Russian search for universal social justice, understood in an extremist sense, and to the Russian method of government and control by coercion. This was predetermined by the whole course of Russian history, but also by the feebleness of creative spiritual power among us. Communism was the inevitable fate of Russia, the inward moment in the destiny of the Russian people.[6]

The Community and the Individual

Here emerges one of the many paradoxes of history. A culture may foster a communitarian ideal—inherently good, inherently Christian—at the expense of that deep personalism which is an essential of all high religion. The paradox often appears in converse form: Accent on the individual person obscures the

---

[5] *Op. cit.*, p. 19. Used by permission.
[6] *Ibid.*, pp. 252-53.

communal element—in Christianity, the *koinonia*. It is perhaps not invidious to point out that Protestantism has often appeared to manifest the latter tendency, and Catholicism the former.

In another passage Berdyaev said of Bolshevism, which, as suggested earlier, is probably the most historically accurate designation of Russian Communism:

> It made use of the Russian traditions of government by imposition, and instead of an unfamiliar democracy of which they had had no experience proclaimed a dictatorship which was more like the old rule of the Tsar. It made use of the characteristics of the Russian mind in all its incompatibility with the secularized bourgeois society. It made use of its religious instinct, its dogmatism and maximalism, its search after social justice and the kingdom of God upon earth, its capacity for sacrifice and the patient bearing of suffering, and also of its manifestations of coarseness and cruelty. It made use of Russian messianism and faith in Russia's own path of development.[7]

In somewhat similar vein, George S. Counts has written that the Bolsheviks have appropriated the

> vision of international revolutionary socialism and have combined it with Soviet patriotism and love of the Motherland, even in some measure with Great Russian messianism. Members of the younger generation have been and are saturated with the doctrine that their country is destined by the laws of social development to lead all mankind to Communism. . . . The appeal has solid foundations in the history of the race and in human society. Even primitive peoples have been known to entertain conceptions of tribal grandeur, superiority, and mission. Practically every political or religious faith during the period of its vitality carries an outward thrust and sends its missionaries to the "benighted" members of the human family.[8]

It is the design and method of this "outward thrust" that is crucial in a moral appraisal of Communist aims.

It would be salutary, no doubt, for us as Americans to consider

---

[7] *Ibid.*, p. 254.

[8] Reprinted with permission of McGraw-Hill Book Company, Inc. from *The Challenge of Soviet Education* by George S. Counts. Copyright © 1957 by McGraw-Hill Book Company, Inc.

in this connection some chapters in our own national history. We have not lacked recurrent moods of expansiveness—a euphemism perhaps for what is now called imperialism. It has been pointed out that at the turn of the century many Americans were preoccupied with the concept of manifest destiny. Even Josiah Strong, one of the pioneers in the movement for the application of Christian ethics to society, had his imagination kindled by what seemed to him the challenge to America to lead the world. This mood found expression in political terms in such statements as the following from Senator Albert J. Beveridge, a contemporary of Theodore Roosevelt:

> The Philippines are ours forever. . . . And just beyond the Philippines are China's illimitable markets. We will not retreat from either. We will not repudiate our duty in the archipelago. We will not abandon our duty in the Orient. We will not renounce our part in the mission of our race, trustee, under God, of the civilization of the world. . . .
> The power that rules the Pacific . . . is the power that rules the world. And, with the Philippines, that power is and will forever be the American Republic.[9]

"Historical Materialism"

Interwoven with the indigenous Russian revolutionary movement was an adaptation of the Marxist philosophy of history and theory of society—historical materialism and the class struggle— and the vision of a world-wide proletarian revolution. Historical materialism in this context connotes the reality and significance of the historic process itself as a nonmechanistic cultural factor susceptible of direction by human effort that operates within the bounds that history establishes, and at the same time the primacy of the material—mainly economic—aspects of human life.

Here was the making of a vast reservoir of power, filled with utopian zeal, bent upon remaking human nature and producing the "new Soviet man." As the power increased and material achievements multiplied, however, the early idealism hardened into political and military dictatorship. The initial vision of a

[9] Quoted by Foster R. Dulles in *The U.S. Since 1865* (Ann Arbor, Mich.: University of Michigan Press, 1959), p. 173.

new world was subordinated to a recrudescent nationalism of the most exclusive type. What was to have been, in the minds of at least some of its leaders, a great demonstration of working-class solidarity and democratic power became a regime directed by a small elite—a new class whose members seem to have sensed the precariousness of their hold, as individuals, on the reins of power and sought to compensate by a ruthless exercise of authority. Conspiracy, always endemic in a dictatorship, became normative as a method in international relations.

To be sure, the Communist dictatorship is in theory a social, collective institution—the dictatorship of the proletariat—and the party is in theory a collective trusteeship for proletarian interests and an executive instrumentality for the working class. Here, in fact, is one of the tension points in Communist theory. Lenin seems to have regarded the leadership of intellectuals as indispensable to social revolution, yet to have believed that leadership is authentic only when truly representing the will of the proletariat. There is room for doubt that Lenin envisaged the totalitarian system into which the movement he led ultimately developed. Indeed, the content of Leninism is an involved and controversial matter. Scholars have reached no consensus on it.[10]

It appears, however, that Lenin's thinking underwent a considerable change under the impact of events. Bertram D. Wolfe, whose comprehensive account of the Russian Revolution has won high praise from critics, has grappled with this problem and analyzed the factors entering into the development of Lenin's thought and strategy.[11] He sees Lenin strongly conscious of the way a political movement is conditioned by the particular historical situation and convinced that Russia was not "ripe" for socialist revolution—as contrasted with the theoretically prior

[10] It cannot be too strongly stressed that wide differences of opinion exist among scholars of comparable knowledge and skill as to the relationship between various strands of the revolutionary movement out of which international Communism emerged. Agreement is lacking, for example, over the content of Leninism as philosophy and political strategy at any one point in its historical development. Indeed, when we speak of "Communism as such" we involve ourselves in a sort of ambiguity which is, however, difficult to avoid.

[11] *Three Who Made a Revolution* (Boston: Beacon Press, 1955), pp. 289 ff.

"bourgeois democratic revolution"—and the bourgeoisie was "too weak and cowardly" to accomplish its own revolution. At the same time he could not countenance nonparticipation by the Social Democrats in any provisional government that might be set up following the fall of the monarchy.

Hence he was confronted by the problem how to keep the revolution democratic, for, says Wolfe: "Lenin in those days was a convinced democrat, and the problem of political freedom concerned him deeply. Not only in those days, but until he seized power in 1917." Later in that year Lenin declared, "Whoever wants to approach socialism by any other path than that of political democracy will inevitably arrive at absurd and reactionary conclusions, both economic and political."

Thus, Lenin the theoretician. Contact with hard realities, as he saw them, later made Lenin the revolutionary leader an uncompromising exponent of "democratic centralism" within a disciplined party in which the theoretical embodiment of the "will of the people" became a fanciful concept reminiscent of Rousseau's idea of the "general will."

Interestingly enough, Lenin's answer to the question he had put to himself concerning the fate of democracy, "Let us take power and then we'll see," was an adaptation of what Wolfe calls Lenin's favorite adage from Napoleon: "On s'engage, et puis . . . on voit." (One commits himself and then . . . he sees.) Here is existentialism with a vengeance!

What seems a considerable ideological difference between Soviet and Chinese Communism has been the tendency in the latter to countenance and encourage a degree of what is commonly called class collaboration. A Chinese Communist statement in 1957, for example, contained this passage: "Even at the present stage of Socialist Revolution, an alliance is still maintained with the national bourgeoisie, their legitimate interests are looked after. . . . For at a certain stage of revolution and under given historical conditions the interests of the working class are identical with the interests of certain democratic classes." [12] The Third Congress

[12] John H. Kautsky, "Neo-Maoism, Marxism and Leninism," *The New Leader* (December 16, 1957), p. 14. Used by permission.

of the Indian Communist Party, in 1953, declared that "the working class must come out for the protection of national industries against the competition of the imperialists." [13] Indeed, Marx himself is on record as saying in 1869:

Once the greater mass of the workers has attained the insight that their material situation must be improved, they may belong to any party they like. For if the material situation of the worker is improved, he can devote himself better to the education of his children, his wife and children need no longer go to the factory, he himself can better cultivate his mind and look after his body, he becomes a socialist without having an inkling of it.[14]

All this is, of course, in marked contrast to the current indications that it is Mao rather than Khrushchev who has been holding to what is regarded as the orthodox Marxist doctrine of the inevitability of the class war. This is a complicated issue, however, to which we shall return later.

The Influence of Nationalism

The role of nationalism, with its emphasis on political and military power, is a rather baffling aspect of the Communist movement. In conception, Communism is international as well as totalitarian; its vision of the future and its purposes are, of course, global. On the other hand, a viable organization of political power, essential to total revolution, inevitably requires a maximizing of the power and influence of at least one national state as an instrument for such an organization of global revolutionary power. This defines the role of the Soviet Union—and apparently of Communist China—in the present world situation.

Conceivably, of course, nationalism may tend to modify the conspiratorial aspect of an international revolutionary movement by emphasizing the traditional pattern of national rivalry and competition. This is not clearly evident at the present stage of the Communist revolution, though in the long run a situation might arise in which serious conflict of interest between the

[13] *Ibid.*
[14] *Ibid.*, p. 15.

39

Soviet Union and Red China would be inevitable. Indeed, there are currently numerous signs of such conflict, but not on a scale that threatens the common front against the West.

In Lenin's time the party emphasized the unadulterated international teachings of Marx and the basic Marxian doctrine of the forcible overthrow of capitalism by an uprising of an organized world proletariat. Throughout the 1920's the Russian words for motherland and patriotism were rarely heard in the Soviet Union, but with the launching of the first Five-Year Plan in 1928 under the slogan "building socialism in one country" the "party line" underwent a sharp reversal. To the astonishment of many Soviet citizens the formerly proscribed words were raised to a position of highest honor. History textbooks were rewritten, the past of the great Russians was placed in a halo of glory, while love of the motherland and burning hatred of Russia's enemies became the basic ingredients of education in Communist morality. The Second World War, in defiance of the tradition of "international revolutionary socialism," is still called "the Great Patriotic War."

The contradiction in this situation is theoretically resolved through the conception of "proletarian internationalism," another powerful ingredient of education in Communist morality and a basic trait of the new Soviet man. Thus the Soviet state proclaims itself the staunch friend and champion of the exploited and oppressed toiling masses throughout the world, and particularly of the peoples living under the "yoke of Western imperialism." It follows that "our truth is the truth of the toilers in all countries," and the historic messianism of great Russia is identified with the Marxian vision of a world-wide proletarian revolution. Significantly, the famous closing words of the Communist Manifesto, "Workers of the World Unite," appear on the masthead of every Soviet paper or journal.

We now see in the Far East the Communist twin of this Bolshevist giant entering upon a similar career, characterized by incredible dynamism, bent both upon making a new man and upon transforming an ancient culture. The Chinese undertaking is in some ways even more audacious than the Russian. To adapt the familiar Churchillian term, there are now two vast Communist enigmas instead of one.

The conflict—actual or potential—between Soviet Russia and Red China in terms of Communist theory is the most conspicuous illustration of a confusing aspect of the Communist movement. That is to say, the setting over against each other of nationalism and internationalism as dominant ideals has pointed up the theoretical issue over the alleged monolithic character of Communism. It is a commonplace that Communism confronts the West as an international conspiracy. The word "international" is commonly used to qualify the word "Communism" when one is preoccupied with the ideological conflict between East and West. Obviously, on the face of it, it seems inconsistent to charge Communism with being an international conspiracy and at the same time to say that our great foe is Russian imperialism—and perhaps potentially China's imperialism. Here, however, we have an illustration of the polarity which commonly characterizes the more serious predicaments in human affairs. If Communism were not an international, global phenomenon, clearly it would not be such a serious threat to Western democracy. At the same time it is evident on every hand that the armed force of a single nation has furnished implementation of the avowed Communist drive to win the minds of men. This problem is commonly discussed in terms of the question whether or not Communism is essentially a monolithic phenomenon. The question is by no means academic, for it bears directly on the all-important matter of a strategy vis-à-vis Communism for the nations committed to Western democracy.

Arthur Schlesinger, Jr., of Harvard, has been very emphatic on this point:

Communism is not a monolith; it is a spectrum. At one end of the spectrum lies China—messianic, austere, passionately ideological, deeply fanatical, and inaccessible to the American observer. . . . At the other end of the spectrum lie Poland and Yugoslavia—countries whose species of Communism confound the clichés which have dominated Western thought in the last decade. In between lies the Soviet Union, the most powerful Communist nation of them all, a singular mixture of excessive confidence and excessive insecurity . . . of extraordinary efficiency and exasperating inefficiency . . . of venturesome innovation and rigid ideology.[15]

Totalitarianism

On the other hand, as has been pointed out many times, Communism wherever you find it is totalitarian and stands in marked contrast to a democratic order and the democratic way of life as these are conceived among us. A bit of analysis seems to be in order here.

1. Within a single nation a Communist regime has a monolithic character in that it attempts to press every aspect of life, secular and religious, into a totalitarian mold. Since human nature has a universal quality and basic human interests are essentially alike the world around, all totalitarian schemes are bound to resemble one another. Arthur Wright of Stanford University has said: "The term 'monolith,' in its contemporary political sense, can be defined as a system in which culture, state, and society are one and indivisible, fused together by common values in all group and individual behavior, enshrined without exception in all institutions." [16] Here we see the aptness of the term as applied to a single state or society. If the word "monolithic" is used in this sense there can be no quarrel with its implication.

2. Modern Communism, like traditional capitalism, is international in that it defines a pattern of life and human relationships which transcends national boundaries. As laissez-faire capitalism, wherever you find it, embodies the same economic philosophy, so it may be said that the several Communist nations are alike in their materialistic philosophy, theory of history, emphasis on class war, and so on. In this respect too Communist regimes tend to be all of a piece.

3. The very existence, however, of nation states with different histories, competing economic interests, and cultural contrasts

[15] "The Many Faces of Communism, Part I: The Theological Society," *Harper's Magazine* (January, 1960), p. 52.

[16] "The 'New China': Myth and Reality; The Chinese Monolith, Past and Present," *Problems of Communism* (July-August, 1955).

makes substantial variety in their social and political systems inevitable. The very fact that "revisionism" has been a bone of contention in Communist circles since Russian Communism undertook to establish itself as an exclusive norm bears testimony to the nonmonolithic character of Communism as a world movement. It can be called monolithic only in a limited sense within a single political entity. Titoism has long been a thorn in the side of the Soviet Union, and latterly it has greatly troubled the Chinese Communists. Yet Tito's regime in Yugoslavia is authentically and dedicatedly Communist, and certainly the same is true of Red China.

The authority of Marx is proclaimed by all Communist regimes, yet Marxism is no longer a definitive term.

Walter Lippmann wrote a few years ago:

What we are seeing is a growing separation between Communism—as an ideology, a secular religion, and a social movement—and the Soviet Union as a great power and an imperial state. In the reign of Stalin the spread of Communism and the increase of the power of the Soviet state were meshed one with the other. . . .

The historic importance of Titoism is that it has been a rebellion against Moscow's use of Communism as an instrument of Russian imperialism. From the end of the World War until Tito's quarrel with Stalin, the Soviet Union treated Yugoslavia as, in the old days, the empires used to treat their colonies: as countries which were not to be developed for their own advantage but were to be exploited for the advantage of the imperial power.[17]

A quotation from a *Wall Street Journal* editorial is interesting in this connection:

We are already familiar with the fact that Yugoslavia, as Marxist as Russia, is no pawn of Moscow; in fact, Titoism has added a new word to the language. And we are beginning to see the first signs—faint though they be at the moment—that being jointly Communist has not obliterated conflicts between Red Russia and Red China. . . .

And let us not suppose that what passes for Communism today in a Congolese jungle is an iron bond with Communism in industrialized,

[17] New York *Herald Tribune* (October 18, 1956). Used by permission of the author.

politically sophisticated Russia; nor that a joint belief in the doctrines of Marx and Engels will submerge the innate clash of interests between black Africa and white Russia.[18]

Another interesting comment on the Yugoslav regime appeared in the October, 1960, *Survey* of the Morgan Guaranty Trust Company:

The system they have built, although differing in both theory and practice from that of any country in the Soviet bloc, is unmistakably Communist. While it offers the window-shopping underdeveloped countries an example not made in Moscow—a distinction that may well prove important in geopolitical terms—it certainly is philosophically closer to Russian doctrine than to American. It allows only one political party, denies private ownership of the means of production, and outlines the national course with five-year plans. But it has wheeled away at a number of points from the Soviet-type system which Marshal Tito installed in Yugoslavia with Russian assistance just after World War II. It is these departures that make the country and its economic performance likely to attract considerable world attention in the future.[19]

Max Nomad, in *Apostles of Revolution,* wrote: "The contradictions abounding in all revolutionary theories are due not so much to deficient logic as to the tactical requirements of the changing political situations necessitating a different approach for the attainment of the same aim—the capture of power. Or else they are due to the changed economic and social status of the victorious revolutionary party." [20] This is an explicit rejection of the monolithic theory.

As between the Soviet Union and Communist China there seem to be two major differences. One has to do with the forced reorganization of social and economic life through the communes —of which the Soviet Union seems to take a rather dim view. The other has to do, as we noted earlier, with the traditional Communist doctrine of the inevitability of war. This was put tersely

[18] (September, 12, 1960). Copyright 1960 by Dow Jones & Company, Inc. Used by permission.

[19] Used by permission.

[20] Boston: Little, Brown and Company, 1939, p. 6. Used by permission of the author.

by Mr. Sulzberger of the New York *Times* when he referred to the assumption in Soviet Russia that the Communist ideology "will triumph by coexistence and has no need for war"; and, on the other hand, to "a ruder interpretation of dogma" which contends that "war is not only inevitable but perhaps necessary." (September 21, 1960.) This should of course not be taken as indicating a rigid or permanent ideological cleavage. It is of the essence of Communistic theory that contradictions are resolved in the historical process. There is reason to think that Marx himself would have had no difficulty in reconciling this one by reference to differences in the particular historical situations in which the two governments find themselves. Indeed, the manifesto promulgated by the Moscow conference of world Communist leaders in December, 1960, contains the remarkable statement that the "coexistence of states with different social systems is *a form of the class struggle* between socialism and capitalism." (Italics added.) This seems to be a formula for accommodation of doctrine and policy to the realities of modern warfare.

There is an interesting passage in a speech by Togliatti, the Italian Communist leader, at a meeting of the Italian Communist Party which is worth quoting here:

> Our distinction between just and unjust wars remains fully in force. ... But if we make the assumption of total destruction, and this applies relatively to both sides, it is quite obvious that other considerations should be added to the definition of the just nature of a war. Let us assume that our country could be hit by the twenty or thirty nuclear charges which would suffice to cause total destruction and transform everything into a desert. Would it be possible to build socialism in those conditions? We should be lying to the people if we said that one could bring socialism nearer through war." [21]

In any case, it seems important to subject the doctrine of inevitability of war to some analysis. It is one thing to contend that armed force is inherently indispensable for the implementation of Communist design and quite another thing to contend that war is inevitable because the privileged classes will never relin-

[21] Quoted by Norman Thomas in a letter to the New York *Times*, August 9, 1960.

45

quish their properties and privileges except as forced to do so by armed might. The former position has affinities with the barbaric notion that war is inherently good because it tends to develop physical or moral perfection in the participants. The latter view maintains that justice can never be attained between social classes except by overcoming possessiveness through force. It may be contended that both these arguments lead to the same end, and therefore there is no important difference between them. This, however, is to overlook the fact that the so-called capitalist order has in recent decades undergone very marked changes which demonstrate, among other things, that privileged classes have actually relinquished advantages and possessions when confronted by a firm consensus, with legal sanctions, and that the hitherto existing distribution of wealth, income, and privilege was no longer tolerable. The mere fact that the concept of the welfare state gained such wide acceptance in the West argues strongly that nations committed to the principle of individual enterprise do in practice accommodate themselves to changes which very considerably alter their status and that of their citizens.

The matter assumes a rather grim aspect in view of the patent difference between the magnitude of the threat of total war to the Soviet Union and the magnitude of a similar threat involving Communist China. G. F. Hudson, a very knowledgeable British interpreter of Far Eastern affairs, has written: "It may well be that Mao Tse-tung really is less daunted by the prospect of a nuclear war because of the vast numbers of the Chinese population and the dispersal of the Chinese economy." [22] It is said that Mao has coolly calculated that even if China became involved in a nuclear war—which is certainly not within the probabilities while she lacks the weapons—even the most disastrous conflict would leave the nation with a relatively large population. This consideration may or may not have influenced the recently announced intention of Mao's government to combat the notion of overpopulation, on the ground that the concept is "fallacious whether applied to China or to any other country." In any case, the fact that Communist China's population is considered to be

[22] "Russia and China: The Dilemmas of Power," *Foreign Affairs* (October, 1960), p. 10.

nearing the 700,000,000 mark and increasing at the rate of 15,-000,000 annually seems highly relevant to this matter. These considerations bear heavily on the apparent meeting of minds at the Moscow conference, above referred to, on the coexistence issue.

As to the difference between the Soviet Union and Communist China concerning the communes, Khrushchev has quite explicitly stated that this degree of regimentation is not practicable. From the Chinese point of view the development of the communes was part of the "big leap forward" whereby the Communist government proposes to reorganize Chinese society. In any case, the project is so radical as to occasion the comment, "The Chinese Lenin has become a Stalin." The commune is a more radical innovation than the Russian collective. G. F. Hudson has said:

With their merging of rural economic units with local state administration, their adoption of a form of military discipline over their members, and their assignment of labor to agriculture, industry or building construction according to the requirements of the planners, China's Communist rulers have achieved a degree of control over their labor force such as not even Stalin was able to attain. Further, the attempt to make distribution in kind the main form of payment to commune members—the system of so-called "free supply"—represents an ambitious move towards the moneyless utopia of pure Communism. Moreover, this occurs at a time when the trend in Russia is in just the opposite direction, toward larger cash incomes for collective farmers.[23]

Incidentally, Khrushchev's conversation with Senator Hubert Humphrey concerning human incentives, as reported by the latter, is hard to reconcile with what is generally understood to be the Communist theory. Speaking in derogation of the Chinese communes Khrushchev said: "You know, Senator, what those communes are based on? They are based on that principle, 'From each according to his abilities, to each according to his needs.' You know that won't work. You can't get production without incentive." [24]

[23] "Mao, Marx and Moscow," Foreign Affairs (July, 1959), p. 567. Used by permission.
[24] "My Marathon Talk with Russia's Boss," Life (January 12, 1959).

Here as always, of course, there is danger in lifting brief statements out of context, but there is more than a hint in what Khrushchev said on that occasion and in the opinions often expressed concerning the Chinese communes by Soviet leaders that the latter consider human motivation very much of a piece, regardless of class. In any case, the distinction now being made explicit between the socialist regime, which the Soviet leaders profess to have established, and the Communist society that is held in prospect is fundamental. It is to the latter that the slogan "to everyone according to his need" is held to be applicable.

The cult of personality of which so much has been heard since Khrushchev launched his attack upon Stalin's record is another example of variety among Communist regimes. Anything in the nature of a personality cult in the Soviet Union would naturally be closely related to the history and assumed destiny of the "motherland" and hence national rather than international. The same may be said for any Communist movement that is bound up with a vigorous nationalism.

The Role of Ideology

An important and puzzling problem has to do with the role of ideology in the growth of Communism and the corresponding importance of ideological instruction in the system of education. There is much difference of opinion on this subject. One of the many scholars consulted in the course of this study contributed the following comment:

It is my impression that the role of Soviet ideology is vastly underrated by the Western world. Even though many ideas have changed, certain basic concepts remain (the same could be said about the history of Christianity). It has been my experience that in this country we seem to be more concerned with Communist methods than in dealing with their ideas. And this is perhaps one of the main reasons why we have been "losing" the Cold War. Relatively few people seem to be willing or able to meet the Communist Gospel in a scholarly, critical, and yet understanding manner, carefully sifting sense from nonsense. Brainwashing at its best is calm intellectual persuasion of the validity of Soviet thought. It often results in a sincere conviction that no matter how many mistakes the Soviet Union makes, it is nevertheless on the right track for purely scientific reasons. It is at this point that our failure to meet the challenge is greatest.

This opinion commands attention. On the other hand Gabriel Almond of Princeton University has called attention to what he calls "the decline of ideology" noted in an intensive study of persons who had left the Communist party, including Americans, British, French, and Italians. He wrote in 1954:

Perhaps the most striking finding as to the differences between the earlier and later generations among our respondents was the decline in the importance of Communist ideology in the processes of recruitment and assimilation. Thus our evidence showed that in the last fifteen or twenty years persons joining the Communist movement have rarely been indoctrinated before joining the party. And, once in the party, the new members are exposed to the ideology under carefully controlled conditions. It comes to them largely in the form of slogans which have to be memorized. Furthermore, the manuals used in this internal party indoctrination are heavily tactical in their emphasis, stressing the central importance of discipline, militance, and activism, rather than of ideals and non-power goals and objectives. Persons leaving the party in this recent period tended to be disillusioned with ideology in general. They tended to become very pragmatic, or completely indifferent, in their political views.[25]

This was found to be in sharp contrast to the first fifteen years of the Communist movement. It invites alternative inferences. One is that the strength of the appeal of sheer social dynamism and momentum has made the earlier elaborate ideological indoctrination seem less important. Another is that ideological fervor was essential only at the stage when the prime need was to fashion a powerful, disciplined, dogmatically rigid leadership composed largely of intelligentsia. A third is the possibility that, as has often been true of revolutionary movements, the *élan* of Communism has begun to weaken and that it is increasingly concerned with power—at the expense of messianism and apocalypse.

[25] *The Appeals of Communism* (Princeton N. J.: Princeton University Press, 1954). p. 396. Used by permission.

The importance of ideology in any mass movement must not of course be underrated. It furnishes a total view of human affairs which makes organization more readily possible. To be sure, it is doubtful if many Communists, even of the more sophisticated variety, comprehend the niceties of Marxist and Leninist thought. It often appears that much less attention is paid by the leaders in their attempts to influence the masses to theory and doctrine than to practical programs. Some observers think that as a movement grows and spreads its ideology becomes less important. Others think differently. A common and serious error is the imputation to Communism of a static ideology.

Communism Hard to Define

It will not be surprising if some readers of these pages are disposed to say to the author at this point, "You have written down a good many items *about* Communism, but why can't you give us a precise definition, which the title of this section seems to promise?" On reflection, however, I hope it will be clear that one purpose of this book is to show why any attempt to frame a precise definition of the movement we are examining is bound to be inadequate and misleading. If a group of leading Communists including, let us say, Russians, Chinese, and Yugoslavs were asked to furnish such a definition the effort would disclose sharp divergence among them. All would agree that Marxism is basic, but there would be dispute as to what constitutes true Marxism and as to which of the Communist parties is really following it. A spokesman for Red China might claim to be a better Marxist than his European comrades, and the Soviet representatives would have difficulty—unless they had been briefed for the occasion by *Pravda* or Khrushchev himself—in explaining the threefold concept, "Marxism-Leninism-Communism." It is safe to say that the Titoists would soon find themselves isolated.

This is a distressing situation for the serious inquirer, yet is it not true that to a secular-minded observer a conference of theologians representing the many strands of ecumenical Christianity would be equally confusing? Perhaps the same might be said concerning a conference representing the several wings of contemporary Judaism. Yet no one doubts the reality of Christianity or of Judaism as a distinctive religious movement of which any student of our culture must take account. It may even be said that the more vital and potent a movement is the more evident will be its lack of a monolithic, and hence readily definable, character. This is but another way of saying that particularity—specific relevance to time and place and cultural milieu—is essential to any dynamic movement.

One distinction, however, should be kept constantly in mind— one that seems to be all too commonly kept out of mind. I refer to the relation between Communism and socialism. It is true that Communism everywhere regards itself as the ultimate form of socialism—a societal pattern in which the basic characteristics of capitalism as it developed in the West will have no place. It is also true, however, that the over-all, ultimate principle to which Communist theory and socialist theory make ultimate appeal has a broad Christian sanction as an ethical ideal. "From each according to his ability; to each according to his need." Yet socialism as a political factor in the Western world is as conspicuously remote from Communism as Communism is remote from Christianity. Democratic socialism, however it may be evaluated, functions within a parliamentarian form of government and attempts to attain its economic ends in and through a democratic political system. There is, therefore, mutual enmity between Western political socialism and all forms of political Communism.

In other words, while a Christian may, on what are to him authentic Christian standards, approve or condemn socialism as he may approve or condemn, by appeal to historic Christian sanctions, any particular economic system, there is fundamental antagonism between Communism as a way of life and as a political system and Christianity in all its forms.

We now turn to a consideration of the reasons why, in spite of this fact, Communism has made so strong an appeal, even to many people who have been reared in the biblical tradition.

3
THE APPEALS OF COMMUNISM

We have learned enough in this study about the nature of the lure of Communism to avoid suggesting that anything can be properly called *the* Communist appeal. It is patent that we are witnessing a drama of global proportions. What has happened in Russia and in China, and what threatens elsewhere, is not to be explained merely by the classic Marxist analysis of social process or the Marxist theory of history. It is highly probable, as already intimated, that a revolutionary period would have emerged regardless of the phenomenal growth of the Soviet Union. The rapid advance of science and technology is a major factor in the political and social upheaval. The population explosion has given rise to a strong sense of urgency in the human situation. Moreover, masses of the world's population, chronically hungry and insecure, have become aware, however dimly, that a new age of potential plenty is dawning. It has been said that we are witnessing a "revolution of expectation." The threat of disastrous pressure of population upon food supply—the Malthusians' grim prediction—is the negative aspect of this outlook, one effect of which is skepticism concerning the adequacy of the classical system of production and distribution. Potential plenty wears an ironic aspect in the light of the wide prevalence of scarcity. We in America speak of "pockets" of economic deficit, but to most of the human race "pockets of plenty" would seem a more appropriate term.

Anti-Colonialism

The role of colonialism in enhancing receptivity to Communism on the part of underprivileged peoples seems to be at an all-time high. It has an ironical as well as a rational aspect since the more enlightened colonial policies have aided in preparing the way for independent nationhood. Indeed, the emergence of "colonialism" as the paramount issue in the 1960 session of the UN Assembly dramatized the East-West conflict in striking fashion. The all-or-nothing crusade against it lacks an adequate rationale, but exhibits—to have recourse to a coined term—a tremendous "emotionale." It is easy to show that the two greatest Western powers have pursued colonial policies which, in spite of some grievous lapses, have made for significant cultural and economic progress on the part of colonial countries, but colonialism has become a symbol of exploitation and aggression. As Nehru has said: "We talk about the crisis of our time and many people view it in different ways. Probably in the U.S.A., the crisis of the time is supposed to be Communism vs. anti-Communism. It may be so to some extent. But the crisis of the time in Asia is colonialism vs. anti-colonialism."

Here again is a complicated and confusing issue, to which further attention will be given in a later section of this report. The point to be made here is that the verbal sponsorship by the Soviet Union of forthright and unconditional abolition of colonialism has greatly enhanced the prestige of the U.S.S.R. in a large part of the world. How quickly the Hungarian slaughter is forgotten!

To the churches it should be clear that the Christian gospel and the far-flung missionary effort of Christianity have given impetus to a restless movement among underprivileged peoples. Indeed, the part played by Christianity in instigating social changes which have ugly unchristian aspects is one of the great paradoxes of history. Yet, to a mind informed by biblical insights this should not be strange. In all human activity good and evil are mixed. The consequences of even the best-conceived reforms have a seamy side. Idealism is often shockingly adulterated in the attempt to implement it.

It should not therefore be too difficult to understand the affirmative response so often given to the Communist challenge by diverse groups and classes in various parts of the world. We in America have been singularly lacking in imagination with respect to it. Inevitably, our most characteristic reaction to the spread of Communism has been one of shock and disbelief. We are accustomed to relative social stability; our pattern of life is comparatively conservative. Furthermore, we have come to identify our economic system with democracy, and currently many identify it with Christianity. This gives our way of life an aspect of permanence, of finality. In contrast, a great part of the world's population has latterly become habituated to social and political instability. Even in a large part of the Western hemisphere political regimes rise and fall in quick succession, and people learn to take revolutions in stride. In Eastern Asia, and currently in the Middle East, revolution has acquired a quality of immanence, and the people seem to take it for granted that social change will come about in more or less catastrophic fashion.

Important also is the fact that Communism organized in a political party that is recognized as wholly legitimate presents a very different aspect from that which it presents as an underground movement. In the United States a person who is believed to be a Communist is suspect; he is regarded as subversive. In contrast, many a country has a sizeable Communist vote, and governments in which Communists hold office are numerous.

One does not have to pursue this subject far to discover that voting the Communist ticket in European or Asiatic countries may indicate little or nothing as to one's political philosophy, but only a practical judgment in a particular situation in which it is believed the Communist party is putting forward the most desirable program or is making an effective social protest. It is not unnatural that a condition of social and economic insecurity or of actual poverty should lead people to make rather desperate choices when governments are being chosen.

This is not to suggest that we are warranted in assuming that poverty and insecurity on the part of the people concerned are the main cause of Communist voting or affiliation with the Communist party. Much has been said and written on this subject, but it is well known that many leaders of the Communist movement throughout the world are themselves not underprivileged or economically insecure. Indeed, it is a matter of common knowledge that the leaders in the revolutionary movements have often come from relatively privileged classes. It is probably true that those who become most passionate in their devotion to a revolutionary cause are restless intellectuals or persons of exceptional gifts whose sensibilities have been outraged by social injustices and the suffering they see about them. This fact, however, in no way lessens the significance of poverty and insecurity as predisposing factors in relation to the Communist appeal to underprivileged peoples.

Hostility to "American Capitalism"

It is also true, embarrassingly enough for us in America, that the global conflict which we call the cold war has tended to build up in the minds of people in so-called uncommitted countries a sense of polarity, in political and social terms, with the Soviet Union and the United States at the opposite poles. Many Christians in European countries who abhor Communism nevertheless take a rather dim view of what is called American capitalism. It is a matter of common remark that the image prevailing in Europe is still the capitalism of the nineteenth century— or perhaps we might say of the period ending with the First World War—whereas in actuality the social-economic picture in the United States has changed so greatly in recent years as to make it questionable whether the word "capitalism" is an appropriate one by which to characterize our present system.

Moreover, disapproval of the United States is no doubt accentuated in some quarters by the tendency to identify freedom and the democratic way of life with a highly individualistic enterprise economy as exemplified in the United States. In recent years flaws in our economic system and our culture have been made conspicuous, not merely by foreign critics but also by socially conscious and influential American citizens. Criticism has been particularly sharp with respect to our pattern of race relations, a matter of crucial importance for American prestige. The Communists have not been slow to make political capital of all this. Uncritical glorification of the Free World and the democracy of the West may actually strengthen the Communist appeal. An attempt to identify freedom, as an ethical and spiritual value, with the American way of life is quite unconvincing to a large part of the human race.

Soviet Achievement

Another important aspect of the matter is the success in economic terms attained by the Soviet Union and, according to current indications, in Communist China. The assumption held in the West until recently, and supported by "conventional wisdom," that the Soviet Union would quickly disintegrate and that Communism would become a negligible factor both politically and economically in international relations has been rudely shattered. It has become startlingly evident that a totalitarian system which is not devoted to what we call freedom can for an indeterminate period accomplish wonders in the field of science and invention. Developments in the Far East within a very few years have completely destroyed the stereotype that has long prevailed in the mind of the West. Indeed, it has been pointed out that the American "image" of the Soviet Union has been significantly altered by what the Russians have lately achieved in the realm of science and technology. We tend to think better of those who turn out to be surprisingly good at what we are good at!

"Idealistic" Appeal

Aside from all these practical considerations, however, we must recognize that the elements, referred to earlier, which Communism in its idealistic form shares with Christianity have made a tremendous appeal to many persons actuated by humanitarian motives. The often repeated remark that Communism is a religion signifies that it is a secular faith which supplies its holder with an ultimate concern and with assurance as to all that seems important to him. Indeed, it seems to him a veritable gospel. The ardent Communist's complete certainty that his cause will triumph—his secular apocalyptic vision—bears more than a superficial resemblance to traditional Christian eschatology. Moreover, one of the most amazing features of the situation we are dealing with is the missionary element in the Communist program. "These Communists," wrote one who has encountered them in the Far East, "believe in missions!" Many a Christian leader has been impelled to exclaim, "If only our people had as much zeal as the Communists!"

With reference to the force of religious training and church affiliation as an antidote for Communist appeal, it must be said that in countries where Communism is a recognized political force religion does not seem to be a potent counteracting factor. Recent studies made in France and Italy of pro-Communist voting on the part of nonparty members have made this clear.

Influence of Religious Background

In his book *The Politics of Despair* Dr. Hadley Cantril of Princeton University has published the results of his extensive inquiry into this subject. Concerning the role of religion he says:

Religion and religious issues seem to be rather dissociated from voting behavior. And the reason apparently is that Communist voters disagree with non-Communist voters on what religion "is." The following figures from a survey made by DOXA in Italy in November, 1953 indicate that the Catholic Church is one thing for the non-Communist Christian Democrat voter and quite another thing for the Communist voter. It is not simply a matter of each having a different attitude toward a church which has certain characteristics. The symbol "Catholic Church" itself has completely different significances for the two groups. . . .

"Do you think a person can at the same time be a good Communist and a good Catholic?"

	Communist Voters	Christian Democrat Voters
Yes	76%	5%
No	13	87
Don't know	11	8
	100%	100%

Quite clearly, it is not difficult for a Communist sympathizer to consider himself a "good" Catholic, and vice versa.[1]

[1] New York: Basic Books, Inc., 1958, pp. 97-98. Used by permission.

The Church and the party, Dr. Cantril concludes, play separate and quite independent roles in such a person's life. He reports further concerning the religious beliefs of Communist sympathizers in the Roman "borgata":

	Communist Sympathizers	Non-Communists
Believe in a hereafter...............	42%	65%
Believe in God.....................	67	92
Believe a *man* should go to church at least once a week...............	56	94
Believe a *woman* should go to church at least once a week.............	80	98
Believe in Jesus Christ.............	69	93
Consider themselves Christians......	78	96
Believe the church is indispensable for serenity and happiness in life..	51	86
Believe priests are useful people....	47	66 [2]

This situation seems to be continuing in spite of the firm stand taken by the Holy See with respect to the Christian attitude toward the Communist party.

Many people would doubtless regard this rather anomalous situation as an indication that religion has but a slight hold on the people in question. This may be true; nothing is more characteristic of the present age in Europe and America than what is commonly called secularism—the denial of the relevance of religion to politics, business, and social life generally. What seems to be a more relevant judgment, however, is that, just as among us in America one's political affiliation is no index to his religious beliefs or the quality of his life, so where Communism is a legally recognized political force the decision whether or not to vote Communist is commonly made on pragmatic grounds. Such political decisions should not be invested with great personal religious significance. To the persons making them it probably never occurs that anything more than a practical political choice is being made in a particular situation, just as

[2] *Ibid.*

millions of ballots are cast in American elections by persons who are conscious of no serious religious or ethical commitment in the act of voting. Moreover—and this is a factor of major importance—in countless situations these pro-Communist voters whose religious beliefs and commitments might be expected to give them pause can find no commendable alternative to the Communist program to support politically. In a "time of troubles" Communism often seems to be, in some parts of the world, the only dynamic force to which to turn. Furthermore, we may well remind ourselves of instances in the history of the United States when our foreign policy called for moral and political support to dictatorial regimes that were incompatible with the political and ethical convictions we profess.

A Close Look at Italy

One of the most ample and astute analyses of this problem elicited by the present study was made by a Jesuit priest who undertook to explain why so many Catholics in Italy support Communism in spite of the position taken by the Roman Church. Because of its thoroughness and candor I am quoting the memorandum at considerable length:

To the question why so many Catholics in Italy support Communism two answers are constantly repeated. It is asserted that they do so because of poverty, or that they do so because of ignorance. Obviously, the two answers frequently appear in combination. Nonetheless, each of the two and the combined answer are equally oversimplifications. But if oversimplifications each nonetheless contains a large element of explanation.

Take first poverty. The oversimplification here is seen at once when it is observed that there are several classes of Italians who are not poor and who nevertheless give their allegiance to the Communist party in one form or another, perhaps principally by voting for them. On the contrary, some of the poorest of the poor have absolutely nothing to do with Communism.

It is interesting to observe that probably none of Italy's 150 Communist deputies [to the Chamber of Deputies] are poor and few are even workers. Most of them would fairly be described as of middle class financial circumstances, provided it be understood that middle class has

59

its lower as well as its higher sectors and that in Italy all of these classes would hardly be well off by American standards. Besides these "middle class" people who support Communism, I would next cite the quite well-off industrial workers of the big industrial cities of the north such as Turin and Milan. These enjoy a level of living far above what they ever dreamed of ten years ago. And yet they continue to belong to the Communist dominated labor union, the CGIL, and to vote Communist even when they don't belong to the CGIL. Such an abomination as Budapest did make an inroad into these ranks, reducing their adherence to the CGIL by some 30 per cent. But even part of that has since been recouped.

Still another class who are not poor and yet adhere to the Communist leadership are those who have recently moved up from the status of dispossessed farm hands to become relatively well-off farmers with a holding of land and a decent house, all thanks to the program of the Christian Democratic government. Close to Rome is a land reform called the Maremma. It is quite a show piece with its well-kept fields and its decent, comfortable, nicely painted houses where once stood only stagnant swamp water. . . .

Into this scene we sent a student to find out what the attitudes of these people were on a variety of questions among which was the Communist party. Imagine the inquirers' surprise when they found that most continued to vote Communist. . . .

It seems to be true that very many of the poorest who should be the most likely victims of Communist propaganda, are immune to it. Why? The answer is that their poverty has always been so unrelieved, so without promise of betterment, that they suppose that the condition they live in is an *inevitable* condition. It is their fate. And so far as many of them are concerned, they have every reason to suppose that it is the fate of all people everywhere, for they do not know that others are better off. . . . Understandably if people accept their poverty as inevitable, they are not prone to accept alluring promises. They simply suspect the stranger and his gilded promises. Quite different is the situation if the wooer can provide a demonstration of betterment. . . . This seems precisely why Italians . . . become targets for Communist propaganda once their economic condition has begun to improve. What takes place here? Their *assumptions* change. They now assume that if they can acquire this present stage of betterment, it is quite possible that they could move up further if it were not for certain *removable* obstacles. These will be economic, social, political. . . .

Am I therefore saying that poverty has nothing to do with people's becoming Communists or Communist supporters? Quite obviously not. For in the case of all the classes I have mentioned in preceding paragraphs poverty, at least *relative* poverty, does play its part.

This is most acutely observable in the working classes including the better-off industrial workers and the underpaid officials of the sprawling government bureaucracy of Rome and the poorly paid school teachers, men heading families for the most part. All of these cling tenaciously to one (and perhaps only one) piece of Marxism. This is that the future of the working class depends upon working class unity. Once the proposition is stated, it can readily be seen that it is less doctrinaire Marxism than it is practical, strategic socialism. One of the most damaging charges which Communist bosses can hurl at defectors is this of breaking working class unity. This is the unforgivable sin for all Italy's leftists right up to the leftists within the Christian Democratic or Catholic party.

The writer of the memorandum believes ignorance to have a paradoxical bearing on susceptibility to the Communist appeal. On the one hand, dense ignorance is a barrier to understanding of, and response to, sophisticated propaganda appeals. On the other hand, relatively ignorant folk are a ready prey to the more elementary forms of Communist persuasion, a major purpose of which is to convince people that it is the capitalists and imperialists who make propaganda against the pure truth of Communism!

An important fact pointed out by the writer is that "in Italy there is no social stigma whatsoever to being a Communist, much less to merely voting Communist. And that even after the revelations of Hungary." Not only so, but there are many areas where "it is the most natural thing in the world to be a Communist."

Coming to the often-heard charge that Communist strength in Italy is due to the "failure of religion" our informant remarks: "Since the Catholic Church is in virtually exclusive possession as the religious force of Italy, if it be true that religion could have been a more vital force in checking Communism, to that extent the Catholic Church must bear uniquely the blame. Nor are there wanting many highly placed churchmen who ask themselves, how have we failed?" He reports, however, that in communities where the influence of religion is vital, Communism makes little appeal.

The "Worker Priests"

Certainly the "worker priests" in France who undertook so dedicated and exclusive a mission to working class people that they incurred disciplinary action on the part of the Roman Church belong in the picture we are trying to draw. We are not here concerned in any degree with the ecclesiastical controversy. A similar one would no doubt have arisen had Protestant ministers been involved. The way in which some of these worker priests in their personal testimony have shown the strength of the appeal of the "proletariat" and of ideas associated with the Communist movement—this is what concerns us. The following passages are quoted from the volume, *The Worker Priests*.[3]

The first is from a statement made by a group of these Catholic priests to their bishop:

We are a group of Catholic priests whose aim and mission is to take part with all our strength in the human and spiritual liberation of the proletariat. The spirit of the Gospel and of Christianity compels us to work thus, towards the unity of all men achieved by the pursuit of charity and justice. It has seemed to us impossible to do so effectively unless our life is linked, in a total community of destiny, with that of the working class. That is why we will never again accept any livelihood other than our wages as workers. That is why we are in unreserved solidarity with all forces representing the working class, unless the means employed should one day conflict with our conscience as Christians or with the true solidarity of all wage-earners.

A city priest writes concerning his conception of the responsibility of a priest: "Doubtless it is his duty—now more than ever —to be in the vanguard of thought and culture. But if all this does not flow from, and does not accompany, a deeper comprehension which makes the priest share utterly and *from within*

[3] John Petrie, trans. (London: Routledge & Kegan Paul, Ltd., 1956), pp. 12, 111, 117-18, 123, 125. Used by permission.

the miseries and aspirations of his companions, they will not recognize him as one of them."

From a priest who was a war prisoner in Germany comes this:

> As I walked through the shops I would see three mates driving rivets with a sledgehammer—a Russian, a German and a Frenchman—and I would admire the faultlessly accurate timing of their movements, the harmonious rhythm of their stroke. Then I would reflect that over and above the contradictions of *Weltanschauung* and incomprehensibility of language, there is an essential bond of labour, and that the common bond of matter is as strong as that of the spirit. The Workers' International is not just a brain-child of Marxism: it is a tangible reality.
>
> This discovery of matter and its unifying function brought me to realise a scale of values I had only guessed at. The hierarchy of work is not just a question of output, authority or even competence. It has a value which is in some sort ontological. I am not speaking now of those who inside the factory are considered as the good workers. Their wages are not always proportioned to their worth. Outside work they may not present a single human quality. They may be stupid, drunken or immoral. In their right place, in the factory, they are, so to speak, transfigured.

The following is from a priest in a thinly populated quarter where lived people of several nationalities:

> These men surrounding me, whom I passed in the street, with whom I would help unload a lorry, with whom I shared the life of labour in the market—I was a loader—these men looked to me neither for advice nor for help. There was only one thing they could feel—we were living the same life and undergoing the same lot.
>
> The world of the workers is no longer without hope. It knows it will break its chains. It knows its oppressors. It believes in a future that will be better because more just. It is ready to devote its richest treasure —its labour—to the service of the community of mankind. Its class-consciousness is not merely negative, but positive. That is what drives it to organise itself, to find leaders and militants—sprung from its own ranks and under their control. Even in the depths of the wretchedest quarters I have never failed to come across some of these militants, these apostles whose whole reason for living was the liberation of their brothers. Nine times out of ten they are Communists. Supported and

guided by the Party, they know they belong to the one force that can change the world. That hope animates their entire life. I thought it part of my mission as priest to share this hope, and to carry the pledged burden of those who were thus becoming its pioneers. So I discovered, not only new men, not only new families, districts and townships, but a *new world*. And I think my priesthood has its place in the world thus being built. . . .

When we got back from the day's work—we were digging a canal— we learnt that the Jugoslavs had been defeated, and that the Germans had invaded Greece. It was as though an extinguisher had been clamped down on us. All of a sudden there was no longer any reason why our captivity should ever end, why we too, like so many before us, should not leave our bones there. At that moment I realised the true nature of the solidarity of the working class, in the conditions it lives under, the exploitation it suffers—the feeling the workers have that it will all have no end, or at any rate that they must not delude themselves with hopes of rapid change.

Startling, but enlightening, these self-revelations tell a story that few of us have ever heard.

"Self-Sacrificing" Communists

Charles C. West, in his uniquely noteworthy book *Communism and the Theologians—Study of an Encounter* offers an impressive interpretation of the Communist appeal in India:

The problem which presents itself to the peasants of India for example is not that of political principle, or even of political freedom, but economic security against the growing pressures of urban manufacturing economy and the centralization of land ownership in absentee hands. For those who have begun to catch a new vision of what is possible in the modern world this grows to the demand for broader opportunity, and a fuller human life. The appeal of Communism to these people lies in its ability to reach their level of concern and give expression to it. Self-sacrificing Communists, largely from other classes, to be sure, live with and organize these people, teaching them, by personal example and confidence, by simple slogans and promises, the fundamentals of the Communist programme. But this programme itself appeals because the Communist Party proves itself to be the one political power which does not compromise with the *status quo;* and which promises to carry through reforms quickly and with force if necessary. This is not necessarily a positive appeal. For many a peasant or worker in such a land, the Communist ideology may be alien and bitter medicine, and the Communists repugnant. His innate shrewdness may even suspect that all is not so revolutionary or so full of promise as appears on the surface, even with these devoted fanatics. Yet even then it may present the appeal of inevitability. It may appear as the only party or organization with the power and inner discipline to bring order in a country out of chaos.[4]

"Stomach" Communism?

The problem is approached from another angle by Gabriel A. Almond:

One of the mistakes of American policy in Western Europe was the expectation that economic aid would by itself lessen the appeal of Communism. What we neglected to consider was the fact that the appeal of Communism in France and Italy is based not so much on the absolute standard of living of the working classes and peasantry, [as] on the great discrepancies between the share of income going to these groups as compared with that going to other groups in the population. Thus the problem in these countries results at least as much from the way rewards are distributed as from the absolute amounts available for distribution.

Even the language used in official statements about the Communist threat in Western Europe reflects this misconception of the factors responsible for the success of Communism. The Communism of these areas has often been referred to as "stomach" Communism. If one has to locate it in an organ of the body, it would be more appropriate to call it "heart" Communism, since what is involved in most cases is not so much hunger, as feelings of rejection and neglect at the hands of a society which gives everything to some and very little to the rest.[5]

There is, of course, another aspect of the matter which transcends material concerns. Among the responses to our inquiry was one from an eminent American philosopher who wrote:

[4] From *Communism and the Theologians*, Charles C. West. © SCM Press Ltd., 1958. By permission of The Westminster Press and SCM Press Ltd.
[5] *Op. cit.*, p. 386. Used by permission.

My judgment is that J. Donald Adams hit the nail on the head when he wrote that "The cold war is fundamentally a battle for men's minds" —a campaign to which the vast flurry and strain over arms and money is *essentially irrelevant*. Whether in advanced or in undeveloped regions, men are moved primarily by their visions, their dreams, their passions. It is, as Camus puts it, the "collective passions of mankind that are now putting the destiny of the whole world at stake." There's a stir abroad, touching imagination through a hope that aspires to be faith, and pinch-hits for faith in its absence. Communism makes its appeal not as an economic doctrine—though its promises of help are always in order —but as a mode of life having a this-worldly eschatology justifying companioned sacrifice. Their drawing power lies in evoking a sense of community in goal and effort, not wholly destroyed by the accompanying whiplash, a sense stirred and nursed along with a skill in showmanship partly meretricious-as-Madison-Avenue, but partly bona fide.

The new Soviet man, wrote Max Frankel of the New York *Times*, "would be a man who places the interests of his society far above his own, who would give not charity but his entire self to the welfare of all. The rearing of such a man, not in samples, but en masse, is at once the dream and justification of Soviet society. Without him, Communists believe, neither their philosophy nor the reality of Soviet life will ever make sense." [6]

That this glorified image has for most of us in the West a spurious ideological taint and is corrupted in practice does not lessen its importance as a factor in the Communist appeal.

Effective Social Reform

More challenging and startling to American Christians is a letter, elicited by the present inquiry, from one of our ablest missionary leaders who served in China. Portions of it follow:

Again and again I heard from my Chinese Christian friends that they had been deeply humbled by the discovery that Communists were really doing the things which they as Christians had merely advocated but never accomplished. And what they had in mind was the abolishment of such evils as Rauschenbusch inveighed against so strongly in the early years of this century, the great disparity between rich and

[6] New York *Times Book Review* (June 14, 1959).

poor in both economic and cultural opportunities. . . .

Communism is proving to be much more of a challenge in the undeveloped countries of the world, precisely for the reason that the evils
inherent in an unregulated capitalistic system, evils largely corrected
by regulation in England and America, are so glaring there. . . .

In the uncommitted countries of the world, if there are still any
persons that can ponder the alternatives in an impartial and rational
way, I imagine that the question shapes in their minds somewhat as
follows: Which system, the democratic or the Communist, will bring
us sooner to the goal of the good society? Will we get there quicker by
retaining a political freedom without economic equality which will allow
us, when we are really for it, to vote in the changes we need, or
shall we sacrifice the political freedom of action in order to get a more
immediate economic good, trusting that somehow, when that good has
been reached and the new social order stabilized, our political freedom
will be restored to us? The values sacrificed in choosing the democratic-
capitalistic system are more immediate and tangible, those sacrificed in
choosing the Communistic system more theoretical and intangible. We
in the West, through long centuries of bitter struggle, have come to
value political liberty too highly to allow it to be sacrificed for any
other purpose, no matter how worthy that purpose might be in itself.
But the newly emerging nations of Asia and Africa do not have that
background against which to weigh the respective merits of political
freedom and the possibility of an immediate economic good.

Background of Revolution in China

I come now, in the laborious process of selecting and organizing material assembled in this study, to a copy of a letter written
in Shanghai in 1925, which throws light on the background of
developments in China in the intervening years which have
shocked and mystified the West. The letter was written by a Christian leader, an American long resident in China, whose sober
wisdom and discriminating judgment I regard as exceptional.
Several paragraphs of the letter follow:

Recently I asked a group of students, leaders in the anti-Christian
organization of an interior provincial capital, what their chief counts
against Christianity were. One after another they spoke enumerating a
dozen or more reasons why they thought Christianity should be opposed.
These charges which they expressed frankly and pointedly centered

around two main objections—those based on materialistic rationalism and those based on an awakened nationalism. Their remarks made up a disconcerting tissue of truths, half truths, misconceptions, and prejudices. Their general position, however, was easily understandable to anyone who tries to see things from the other man's point of view.

Christianity, they said, is dogmatic, irrational, in conflict with science, superstitious, opposed to progress. Whatever grounds there may be for these charges are magnified in the Chinese mind which has historically been social rather than theological in its interests. The critics of Christianity moreover naturally judge it in terms of actualities which they see, not in terms of unrealized ideals. They see organized Christianity represented in China under one hundred and forty different labels, divided by differences in dogmas and practices which are meaningless to the uninitiated. This chaotic condition in the Church sadly weakens it as the exponent of a spiritual view of life which it should be presenting in sharp opposition to the stark materialism widely preached in China at present. "Karl Marx has more disciples in China than Jesus Christ," a government school principal said to me sometime ago.

The most vigorous attacks on Christianity at present, however, are expressions of the rising tide of nationalism which, sweeping around the world, has engulfed China. The anti-Christian movement is in certain important aspects a Chinese counterpart to American Ku Klux Klanism. "Christianity," say its critics, "threatens the political and cultural integrity of our nation. It serves, though at times unconsciously, as the agent of Western imperialism—political, commercial, and cultural. Has not the murder of missionaries been used as an excuse for robbing us of our territory? Missionary propaganda and trade expansion have gone hand in hand. Missions, especially mission schools, have by subtle processes of 'cultural penetration' sought to overthrow our ancient civilization and to substitute therefor a civilization which the European War has made us loath to accept." . . .

Great Britian has had to pay for her long ascendency in Far Eastern affairs by being singled out as the arch-offender against China's rights. It is impossible to understand the present situation except in terms of War. China and Great Britain have been engaged for the past two months and more in War. It has been an economic war and not a war of armies and navies. Apparently, however, the same sort of propaganda is required to maintain both species of war. The familiar psychology of 1914-18 quickly appeared. Opinions have been sharp, absolute, intolerant. One's own side has been absolutely right and the opposing side, therefore, absolutely wrong. The way of the neutral has been hard.

Partisans have insisted that "those who are not for us are against us." The Chinese have closely scrutinized their missionary acquaintances to see whether their primary loyalty in this crisis is to Christ or to Caesar. Foreigners have been equally quick to detect "defection" in their ranks expressed in sympathy with the Chinese cause; "anti-foreign foreigners" is the special term of opprobrium which has been coined to stigmatize such. This, by and large, has been the general situation.

Here is a record of cold war before the cold war—before the Communist conquest of mainland China was dreamed of in the West.

An educator reported on his experience in Shanghai in 1946 with a group of college students who had been active in their Christian associations and who were eager to help the Chinese people. Among their activities were informal teaching of illiterates to read and write and efforts to establish co-operatives among farmers and industrial workers.

He wrote:

These efforts were nipped in the bud by Nationalist authorities and particularly by the Deans of Discipline appointed to each private and national university by Nanking on the ground that they were "currying favor with the masses"—a Communist technique—and that if they continued they would be considered Communists and treated as such.

Because of this and other similar pressures they reported, they were pushed much further to the left than they would have liked since the only other alternative was to give up what they believed was their Christian and their patriotic responsibility and obligation.

Similar reports came from students in other parts of the country when we were visiting the various Christian universities. I am reasonably sure that such policies did push many important individuals and groups into the arms of the Communists.

There is no way of weighing such factors in relation to others, but they undoubtedly played a part—largely overlooked—in fostering an attitude in China that was later to cause surprise and dismay in the West.

The testimony of Whittaker Chambers in his book *Witness* concerning his conversion to Communism is a striking illustration of the appeal to which many young idealists have responded:

The ultimate choice I made was not for theory or party. It was . . . a choice against death and for life. I asked only the privilege of serving humbly and selflessly that force which from death could evoke life, that might save . . . what was savable in a society that had lost the will to save itself. I was willing to accept Communism in whatever terms it presented itself, to follow the logic of its course wherever it might lead me, and to suffer the penalties without which nothing in life can be achieved. For it offered me what nothing else in the dying world had power to offer at the same intensity—faith and a vision, something for which to live and something for which to die. It demanded of me those things which have always stirred what is best in men—courage, poverty, self-sacrifice, discipline, intelligence, my life, and, at need, my death.[7]

Workers' Opinions

In Hadley Cantril's book, quoted earlier, he includes some sample opinions obtained during the conduct of his study several of which it seems appropriate to quote in this report.

Here is a summary opinion of a group of French workers:

The workers themselves look upon the employers as continuously working against their interests while favoring the interests of their relatives and those in their own social class. Yet the resentment is not so much against the patron as it is against the "system" for allowing such a state of affairs to exist. The workers put the situation this way: the state allows the patron to skim the milk, leaving very little for the workers.[8]

The following is from the editor of a leading French daily:

Suppose you are a worker in France: you do not have a car as the American worker does or a small flat with a living room and bathroom as the English worker does. You live in a slum with no modern conveniences; your work may be as much as twelve miles away. Your wife can't make ends meet. You feel isolated by the political system in power,

---

[7] New York: Random House, 1952. Used by permission. This quote appeared in *Know Your Communist Enemy. Who Are Communists and Why?* Published by the Office of Armed Forces Information and Education, Department of Defense, 1955.

[8] *Op. cit.* p. 56. Used by permission.

with its press, radio, and military strength. You try to join with other workers to make this system seem a little less frightening. This is where the Communists come in. It appeals because it seems to provide some form of security which can protect workers when they need it. But if workers could find some other strong movement to support which was also against the system, they would shift away from Communism tomorrow.[9]

An Italian farmer is quoted as saying, "When I work with the Communists, I have the satisfaction of feeling that I have become a part of a great mass movement working for a better social order."

Dr. Cantril comments:

For most French and Italian workers, the "something" that is "wrong" is identified with and focused upon the "system," the state and the ruling class. While the vast majority of both French and Italian workers do not seem to feel any strong desire to revolt or to engage in violence against anything specific, there is a consistent disparaging reference in the interviews to what is regarded as an outmoded economic, political and social system. This resentment becomes increasingly bitter with the growing realization of the possibilities for a better life that modern technology provides some people and could provide a much larger number of people if only somehow the "system" were different.[10]

The following statement by a teacher in a French technical school is of rather curious interest:

When you look at present-day society, you can't help judging that the capitalist system is unhealthy and that it has to be discarded. Obviously you can't create a revolution overnight. But only the Communist Party holds out the hope of bringing it off. For me, the Communist Party is essentially an economic party which means to change the economic regime. Communism works for the same goal as Christianity, but on different levels, mainly for the emergence of man.

I may even join the Communist Party sometime. I am not sure because I know there is danger of being pulled along by the atheism of the comrades and by the materialistic philosophy. But I will still vote

[9] *Ibid.*, p. 56.
[10] *Ibid.*, p. 55.

for the Communists because it is the best way to express myself politically and socially.[11]

Variant Views

The following excerpt from a communication received from a religious leader in Scotland is highly relevant to our inquiry. The writer regards the trade unions as the chief target of the Communist's persuasive efforts. He writes:

They only get away with it, of course, because of the appalling apathy of the average trade union member—and the more appalling apathy of trade unionists who are members of the Churches. Communists are usually most efficient trade unionists with a sound knowledge of union constitutions, practice and procedure and rule books about which Christian trade unionists are in the great majority of cases as ignorant as children in Primary School. The Communists too are aggressive and swift to make a show of standing up for "justice" for their fellow trade unionists. Moreover, it is not just because Christian trade unionists are ignorant about trade union affairs and therefore timid and inarticulate, but also because they share in the deep underlying hostility to management, that they allow Communists to take the lead in demands for increased wages, etc., and are party to strikes which set the rule book and agreements at nought. Elders of the Church of Scotland have been reported to me as saying on several occasions things like, "Well, if the Communists are going to get me ten bob a week more, I'll vote for the Communists"—ignorant or regardless of the fact that the Communists are following the Party "line."

In an article in the magazine *Middle Eastern Affairs* Joseph S. Berliner, economist of Syracuse University, wrote:

Why, it is sometimes asked, have the non-Communist underdeveloped countries been such easy targets for Communist economic penetration? Is it because of ignorance of Soviet subversive objectives, or is it some dark oriental propensity for committing national suicide? In evaluating the success of the Soviet credit and trade program, it is important to keep in mind that the image of the U.S.S.R. in the underdeveloped

---

[11] *Ibid.,* p. 87.

countries is rather different from that held in the West. On the one hand, to be sure, there are memories of the Stalinist years when the domestic Communist parties of Asia were committed to a policy of militancy and violence, when Nehru was characterized in the Soviet press as an imperialist tool and Nasser as a fascist usurper. But this face of world Communism has changed since the death of Stalin.[12]

Intellectual Appeal

Herman F. Reissig of the Council for Social Action (United Church of Christ), in the course of an article, "The High Price of Peace in Our Time," has the following to say about the nature of the Communist appeal:

> For the first and only time in human affairs, Marxism-Leninism gave to the world: (1) a coherent analysis of the growth and character of social institutions, (2) an over-all structural blueprint of a new social order, including an ethical goal, economic and political organization, and cultural character, and (3) an apparatus and methodology for bringing the new order into existence.
>
> This combination of philosophy, goal, and working plan has a coherence and depth that appeal to the intellect. It has attracted humanitarians through its radical rejection of poverty and exploitation and its high goal of a society in which all work together for the good of all. It appeals to the victims of poverty and injustice because it recommends, not patience or submission, but quick and radical reform. . . .
>
> To be sure, original Marxism-Leninism is now overlaid with motivations and historical developments, which appear to most of us to have all but smothered its genuine humanitarian aspects. . . . I am speaking here, not about the motives of the Moscow and Peiping governments, but about the attraction that communism has for the restless people in the new nations.[13]

The Moral Appeal

A correspondent in the Far East contributes the following bit of interpretation:

> I think that one thing about the Communist program which appeals, and it inspires the idealism of youth, is the social betterment program

---

[12] August-September, 1959, p. 289. Used by permission.
[13] *Social Action* (May, 1959), XXV, No. 9, 9-10. Used by permission.

which they carry on. In spite of the fact that I felt the tragedy of the over-all situation, I could not help admiring many things the Communists did. The Chinese Nationalist Government had talked about helping rural people in such things as health, literacy, et cetera. They had undertaken small programs, but within months of taking control, the Communist Government was already doing more than the Nationalist Government had ever done in this field. Of course, it was partly because of their system that they could place workers in the country whether they wanted to go or not, but the fact remains that they trained workers to go to the country to help in health matters, and to teach literacy. The Communist Government bookstores were full of very attractive, simple books on health, sanitation, and many other subjects, as well as the large number of purely political books. The Communist workers really sacrificed personal comfort in order to help the people. . . . For example, during the time when fighting was going on in North China, the Nationalist armies often lived off the country. Each Communist soldier had to carry a certain amount of grain, and could never take anything from the people unless it was paid for. . . . Later the disillusionment came when the farmers found that the grain levies were very high, and even later when many had land taken away from them, but in the beginning the reaction was favorable, which is the reason there was so little resistance when [the Communists] took over.

One of the most striking statements concerning the impact of the entrance of Communists into China is the following report by a prominent missionary leader:

Before the actual establishment of the Communist regime, Christian pastors, influenced partly by the brutal excesses of Communist armies in earlier years, and partly by the prevailing attitude of the West, with which they were in contact through the missionaries, had been accustomed to look upon the Communists as people of low moral character with an unbridled lust for power and no regard for the rights of other people. They were accordingly amazed to find them a party with a highly developed moral sense and a deep sense of dedication, which led them to self-sacrifice and self-discipline of so thoroughgoing a nature as to shame the Christians who had formerly thought of themselves as the only ones in China willing to sacrifice for their ideals. The shock of this realization was devastating.

An Orthodox Church Proclamation

In November, 1959, a proclamation was addressed to the heads of the autocephalous Orthodox churches by the chief authorities of the Orthodox Church in Soviet Union concerning the Soviet disarmament proposal. It is illuminating in this context:

God-enlightened Priors of Holy Churches of Our Lord, greeting you from the bottom of our hearts, we, Patriarch Alexius of Moscow and All Russia, together with the Holy Synod of the Russian Orthodox Church, address Your Beatitudes, intending to state our attitude to the proposal of the Government of the Soviet Union for general and complete disarmament.

It is no exaggeration to say that this proposal is the most outstanding event of our time. It focuses the attention of all peoples yearning for deliverance from the fear of war; involuntarily our Christian hope and prayers for the "peace of the world" are associated with it. Therefore, we servants of the Church, preaching the Gospel of peace in Jesus Christ (Acts, 10:36), must say our word in defense and support of the hope inspired in men by the possibility of general and complete disarmament.

To us Orthodox Christians of the Soviet Union this proposal of our government represents an expression of the sincere desire to deliver mankind from the threat of a new world war. We see in this plan a true way for a real improvement of international relations which are continually darkened by the fatal competition in armaments. . . .

The fact that the Soviet proposal for general and complete disarmament is in harmony with Christian faith offers encouraging hope that the Western powers will carry it out in the spirit of Christian trust.[14]

One may question, of course, whether such a statement would have been promulgated by these spokesmen for the Russian Church had it been proposed after Khrushchev's performance at the October, 1960, meeting of the General Assembly of the United Nations instead of following his earlier visit to the United States and the birth of "the spirit of Camp David."

Authoritarianism and False Security

Interestingly enough, it has been suggested that one reason for

[14] Copyright 1960 Christian Century Foundation. Reprinted by permission from *The Christian Century*.

the strength of the Communist appeal is the very characteristic of the movement which invites the sharpest criticism in the West, namely, its authoritarianism. It is pointed out that many people are happiest under authoritarian government, and this is true in an ecclesiastical as well as a political context. It would seem highly probable that in the unsettled state of the world which has prevailed now for many years, a sense of uncertainty and insecurity would lead many to look for guidance to sources that offered the greatest degree of assurance. Very much is made by Christian theologians of the certainty of the ultimate eschatological triumph of the will of God and its redemptive purpose for the world.

At this juncture no confident appraisal of the persuasiveness of such certainty in Communist doctrine is possible. What is in question here is, of course, of the most fundamental importance, philosophically and practically. Perhaps the most that can be said is that the answer to the question thus raised depends upon the relative numbers of those who feel the urge to freedom and independence and those who yearn for certainty.

The question gains significance from the evidence that Communists put forth such tremendous efforts to mold the minds of the young, to develop a new type of personality, and to alter in fundamental ways the social and political order. If a vast enthusiasm can be generated for conformity to a pattern that is supported by high authority and prestige, it is an open question whether what we in the West regard as a native, human urge to be free will assert itself in the face of the manifest success of an authoritarian regime which "delivers the goods" in terms of elemental human needs and wants.

Michael Polyani has recorded a striking confession on the part of a Hungarian former Communist who was later executed for his participation in the uprising of 1956. He wrote:

Slowly we had come to believe, at least with the greater, the dominant part of our consciousness we had come to believe, that there are two kinds of truth, that the truth of the Party and the people can be different and can be more important than the objective truth and that truth and political expediency are in fact identical. This is a terrible thought, yet its significance must be faced squarely. If there is a truth of a higher order than objective truth, if the criterion of truth is political expediency, then even a lie can be "true," for even a lie can be momentarily expedient; even a trumped-up political trial can be "true" in this sense for even such a trial can yield important political advantage. And so we arrive at the outlook which infected not only those who thought up the faked political trials but often affected even the victims; the outlook which poisoned our whole public life, penetrated the remotest corners of our thinking, obscured our vision, paralysed our critical faculties and finally rendered many of us incapable of simply sensing or apprehending truth. This is how it was, it is no use denying it.[15]

There is more difficulty here than meets the eye, for even in the morality of the West sanction is given to the telling of an untruth as a means of winning a wartime objective, and many a conscientious person has struggled with the problem presented by a situation in which the telling of literal truth might inflict grievous suffering or even death upon an innocent person. Moreover, when we make an adverse judgment, as we must, upon the way in which members of Communist parties play fast and loose with the truth we should not be unmindful of the fact that some of our own philosophers take a position with reference to objective truth which is not far removed from that represented in the Communist ethic. The ultimate question here is the perennial one of the relation of means to ends, to which we shall have occasion to refer in a later section.

[15] *Beyond Nihilism* (London: Cambridge University Press, 1960), pp. 31-32. Used by permission.

4
COMMUNIST METHODS
OF WINNING SUPPORT

In the following discussion, as in what has gone before, we shall be concerned with the impact, both direct and indirect, of Communism upon Christianity. By direct impact I mean the effect of face-to-face encounter between the Communist "apparatus" and Christian institutions or persons who give allegiance to Christianity. By indirect impact I mean the effect which Communist activity has had on any or all phases of community life, religious or secular, in which Christianity by the very nature of its message and its mission has something at stake. If Christians are "converted" to Communism, thus effecting a shift in spiritual allegiance, the loss to the Church is obvious. Not always so obvious is the effect upon the Church of Communist inroads upon those secular institutions, public or private, whose character and purpose in considerable measure reflect the biblical tradition.

This section is inevitably a projection of the preceding one; it reports on ways in which the contrived appeals of Communism are brought into play. Like the appeals themselves, the methods are diverse and often of contrasting and even contradictory import. Also, they range from a conspiratorial and deliberately deceptive character to a convincingly sincere effort to further ends which are quite compatible with Christian ethics, if not with the Christian faith. It has surely been evident to the reader that this entire discussion presupposes a mixture of values in the Communist movement. We shall never be able to confront it if we assume that it is totally evil, that every Communist activity is conspiratorial and every program subversive. It is a strange thing that those interpreters of Communism who regard it as evil *in toto* miss the appalling implications of such a judgment, for if a movement that is utterly pernicious can "sell" itself to hundreds of millions of people, hope for the human race is slender indeed, and government by the people is a weird dream. It cannot be too strongly stressed that the major moral hazards that imperil human life, individually and collectively, are compounded of good and evil, life-affirmation and life-denial. This is implicit in the biblical conception of life. Oddly enough, there is more than a hint of it in the Marxist philosophy, with its emphasis on "contradictions" and the "interpenetration of opposites." If, in man's traffic in values, evil and good were separately packaged, the moral tragedies of history would presumably be few. By the same token, however, the meaning of freedom would be small.

It has seemed appropriate thus to preface the discussion of Communist methods and tactics because of the inevitable tendency inherent in the cold war to regard every word and act of the "enemy" as suspect and to assume the worst, as a matter of protective strategy. This shows the basic difference between peace and war: In peace, the presumption of innocence is paramount; in war, the presumption of the adversary's total guilt prevails. If a transition from war—cold or hot—to peace is to be effected, this sort of absolutist, black-and-white appraisal will have to be discarded.

It would go without saying, perhaps, that all Communist strategy is linked, in theory or practice or both, to the use of military force as a necessary potential resource. War is assumed in strict "anti-revisionist" doctrine to be always a possible necessity, and this on two levels. The war of class against class is the basic conflict; wars between nations are assumed to arise out of the class struggle because capitalism is international in essence, and capitalistic states—as "executive committees" of the capitalist class within those states—make war on each other as economic interests dictate. Capitalistic states will, on this theory, make war on a socialist state, using war as an instrument of class policy. (The present military stalemate or *détente* is due to the superimposition of a nonpolitical, nonideological factor upon the historical situation, namely, nuclear energy and "ultimate" weapons.) All this is peripheral to classical Communist theory, however—just as the involvement of the West in global war was not implicit in democratic theory. Since we are here concerned with Communism regardless of the "accidents of history," we may for the present disregard the resort to war as an instrument of Communist policy.

It should be said, however, that the much-discussed Communist design for a world state conceals a very considerable ambiguity. The common tendency to explain all Communist strategy and tactics by reference to an attempt at world domination by one or more powers confuses the situation. John Courtney Murray, S. J., has put this point forcefully:

> It is not enough to cite as the single characteristic of the Soviet empire that it is intent on "world domination," and to let it go at that. . . . The trouble is that the stock phrases tend to become simply incantations. They are invoked as curses on the enemy or as cries of alarm to sustain a mood of fear and opposition. So it is with the phrase "world domination." It has ceased to yield any clear demonstrable meaning. It has even acquired false connotations, as if the primary Soviet aim were domination by military conquest.[1]

"International Communism" is a class conception primarily, and only secondarily a nationalistic conception. That is to say, the foundation of the projected world revolution as Communism conceives it is the proletariat of the world, and hence the primary struggle is between the working class and the capitalist class. As the state in a Communist country is in theory the political instrument of the party, so it would seem that the world federation would be an instrument of an international proletariat. The Soviet Union's persistent opposition to the idea of a super-state indicates that—again, in theory—its goal is a fusion of classless nations rather than a conquest in the historic pattern.

Communist strategy and method in the effort to win support and establish control fall into two general categories, depending on the legal status of the Communist party: (1) In countries that condemn and penalize Communist activities; and (2) in

---

[1] Walter Millis and John Courtney Murray, S. J., *Foreign Policy and the Free Society*, Fund for the Republic, Inc., 1958, p. 21.

those which assume a permissive attitude toward the Communist movement. We have already referred to the legal status of Communism in a given country as a factor in susceptibility to its appeals. This matter must be kept constantly in mind as we consider methods and stratagems. For us in the United States it is extremely difficult to conceive of the Communist movement as it is thought of in most of the other nations of the world, for although our State Department classifies this country as one of those in which Communism is not outlawed, the movement is, both in law and in custom, placed in the category of subversive conspiracy. That it has a conspiratorial aspect is plain enough, but the point is that when one is concentrating on Communism as an international conspiracy simple, common-sense judgments tend to be inhibited. He must change his focus in order to see, behind and beneath the ugly and ominous aspects of Communism, the convulsive upheaval of revolutionary forces that are not merely contrived by plotting conspirators but are mass phenomena that have more dynamism than rationality.

With these distinctions in mind we may proceed to a consideration of various ways in which the Communist "apparatus" operates. No attempt at a survey will be made. The purpose of this section is rather to note different types of method and tactics for the light they throw on the ethos of Communism and on problems of effective response to the Communist challenge.

Propaganda

Far and away the most powerful instrument of Communist power is propaganda. Once it might have been said that military might was the number one weapon for the spread of Communism, and it still remains highly probable that without the Red army the Soviet Union would be unable to keep its grip on its satellite empire or to maintain its enormous influence in world politics. The long-run efficacy of military might maintaining dominance, however, is always dependent on ability to control without engendering so much hatred and non-co-operation on the part of the peoples concerned as to frustrate the purpose of the dominant power. Here is where propaganda becomes vital. Today the short-run potency of military power is progressively curtailed because the great god Mars has developed suicidal mania. Even in former times propaganda—both on the home front and across the enemy's lines—was a major weapon, but in our time it is demonstrating a paramount potency.

There has been long dispute over the definition of propaganda, especially in relation to the concern among psychologists and educators for "propaganda analysis." In general, it seemed to be agreed in theory that propaganda is not necessarily evil—that it is good or bad according as its aims are legitimate and its method honest. The tendency in practice, however, has been to use the word in a pejorative sense, as designating something sinister and reprehensible. In the present world situation, it is clear that just as in the waging of actual war the use of propaganda is subject to no other criterion than that of immediate effectiveness, so in a world divided into hostile camps propaganda has little more conscience than bombs. Moreover—and this is the crux of the matter—effective propaganda in international relations is a behavioral composite: It is a combination of communication and overt acts which conveys to those at whom these are directed a vivid impression that the nation behind them is one that it pays to have as friend or ally, or both—and not one to have as an enemy. The attempt in the West to counter what is to us obviously phony propaganda of friendly words by demanding deeds to back them up is logically flawless, but practically it is in great part futile. Khrushchev knows what he wants and whom he wishes to impress. What we called "antics" and vulgar showmanship in his performances in the UN Assembly may not, on balance, have made a "credit" entry in the Premier's diplomatic ledger, but the havoc he wrought in the Assembly was ample testimony to his influence on the group of new nations whose recent admission to the UN has profoundly changed the political balance of the organization. A broken pledge or a specious argument may at the time take a heavy toll of a statesman's reputation, but as in the case of discarded platform declarations by our own political parties, all is forgotten if, on balance, the "goods" delivered give satisfaction. An editorial in *Pravda* at the time of Khrushchev's performance entitled "The Verdict of History," declared that his words demanding the liquidation of colonialism would be "written in golden letters."

A salient feature of this revolutionary era, as of any "time of troubles," is a greatly increased discrepancy between principles professed and methods employed to achieve what are held to be all-important ends. Related to this is the erosion of mutual confidence in the relations of governments. Consider, for example, the tragic course of the Korean War—the hatreds it engendered and its legacy of distrust and recrimination. What is of practical import now is not that the United States and the United Nations had a rationale for every aspect of policy adopted, but that the enemy was able to discredit it. The most grievous example is continued "coexistence" of a conviction in the West that Red China made war on the UN—a crime of which that government is still unpurged—and the counter belief, not without a measure of support in the West, that the crossing of the thirty-eighth parallel by UN troops was an overt act of aggression against which Communist China had repeatedly warned.

It is not words, but events shot through with ambivalence and ambiguity, that constitute the hard core of propaganda. The moralistic attack on false propaganda tends to be ineffectual because the complex of interrelated events lends enough obscurity to the issue to cast doubt upon any objective judgments that may be pronounced. Just as the meaning of authority depends on its acceptance for action, so the significance of propaganda is not in its integrity or falsity, but in the degree of plausibility that leads to its acceptance. Propaganda, however it may be deplored by high-minded persons, today constitutes a major part of public relations between nations. Characteristic of its use is the maximizing of what it is believed will make for a good reputation and promote the national interest, with omission, rationalization, or outright denial of everything, however true, that will presumably have the opposite effect.

Not a word of this discussion should be taken as condonement of the deception which is practiced in the name of diplomacy and which the Communist governments have patently developed in expert fashion—as the Nazis did before them. It remains true, however, that while Christian ethics does not exempt nations any more than persons from moral obligation, no great nation even approximates, in policy or in conduct, the New Testament standard, and *all* have to settle for a *modus vivendi* rather than a covenant that will guarantee all-round exemplary performance. This is why there is a stalemate in disarmament negotiations and in other aspects of the cold war. In a time of greatly accelerated social and political change it is from a practical point of view—that is, in the interest of averting disaster—virtually irrelevant to seek agreement on the "truth of the matter" with respect to bitterly contested issues. The propaganda war will go on, with East and West deeply involved in it, until some mutually acceptable status is achieved—one representing a maximum of attainable advantage and minimum damage to each side.

"Infiltration"

That a major instrument of Communist policy is clandestine infiltration of agencies of government and nonpublic organizations is too patent for argument. We are concerned with it here, of course, as an instrument of policy only where a non-Communist or an anti-Communist political regime obtains—that is, where it has a subversive character. For present purposes infiltration may be defined as the "planting" of Communist agents in positions where they are assumed to be serving as loyal employees or volunteers, but where they secretly serve Communist purposes. They may or may not be "card-carriers." It appears to be a party policy in some circumstances to use as agents persons who are not party members in order to avoid possible disclosure. For this reason the mere declaration "I am not a Communist" or "I have never been a Communist" is not necessarily enlightening.

It is important to distinguish between infiltration in this sense and other forms of Communist or pro-Communist activity because the "planting" of an agent, who is in the first instance a Communist, in a religious, educational, or other type of organization is really a form of espionage, not different in essence from the same procedure where a government agency is involved. Detecting such activity in a church agency, an educational institution, or other voluntary organization is an expert's task—the kind for which FBI agents are trained. If a Communist secret agent is discovered to be at work in such capacity it is of course gratuitous to hold the agency or organization concerned responsible for his treachery.

There is no reason to think that in this country infiltration of churches or religious agencies by Communists has occurred to any significant degree. In his comprehensive study *Communism and the Churches* Ralph Lord Roy presents evidence of a limited amount of such activity. He cites the Communist *Daily Worker* as reporting in 1935: "The YCL [Young Communist League] in the U.S. has gone directly into the Y's, settlements, churches, and there reached the masses of youth that are not yet organized into unions and sport organizations." [2] Roy records other instances, mostly involving Negro churches, where Communists practiced infiltration, ostensibly out of concern for better race relations. Such efforts were, on the whole, without substantial results.

Information received from abroad, however, in the course of the present study indicates that infiltration of churches has not been infrequent. A prominent missionary leader wrote that he had been "assured" that a Chinese synod in Indonesia had been "undermined and infiltrated" by Communists.

Another missionary who had worked in the Far East wrote, "There is every reason to believe that attempts have been made and are being made to plant Communists in responsible positions on staffs and boards secretly, in order to poison the minds of the people."

From another source comes the following observation:

After the Communists were in power they appealed to "patriotic Christians" to unite with the whole of the people to defeat imperialism, which included in practice the ejection of Westerners from the country and from positions they had in the churches. In Peiping the Communists saw to it that they had representatives in every religious body secretly reporting to them about the political attitude of the church-goers.

[2] New York: Harcourt, Brace & World, Inc., 1960, p. 102. Used by permission.

Obviously, it is a simpler matter to infiltrate educational and social service institutions and agencies than to plant party agents in specifically ecclesiastical offices. As one of our best informed correspondents put it, on the basis of observations in various regions: "I would doubt very much if attempts were ever made to 'plant' Communists in responsible positions on staffs of boards or churches. It is incredible to me that such would have ever been possible, or that anyone would think it was. What may have happened in some instances is that individuals already in responsible jobs may have been influenced by Communists." Although there is, as noted above, some contrary testimony, it seems highly probable that what is indicated in the last sentence of this quotation is much more common than infiltration.

Communism Portrayed as Ethically Christian

Here again is a method that is sometimes used vigorously and effectively, and sometimes avoided altogether. Strategy is determined by reference to the immediate situation. An impressive account of missionary experience at the time of the Communist conquest of China was given us by a veteran missionary. It warrants quoting at some length:

We were in Peking. The Communist armies under the red Napoleon, Chu Teh, were sweeping down after their conquest of Manchuria, across the rich plains of Peking, closing in for the kill on that ancient city. We had to decide whether to evacuate or to stay. Along with many other missionaries we decided to stay. . . .

I had been asked to teach at a university nine miles outside the Peking city walls. We raced to get there ahead of the Communists, along roads that were packed with Nationalist troops retreating in wild disorder. A lieutenant galloped up to us, waving a pistol, and shouting, "Look out, get back into the city, the Communists are around the corner and they will kill you." . . .

We were confused, we were panicky, we were frightened. The bloodthirsty conquerors of Manchuria were upon us. The next night the Communists came in—but not at all in the rude, bloodthirsty way that we had imagined. It was one of the shocks of my life, the next morning, to go out of the house and discover the Communists in their dirty, padded, mustard-yellow uniforms, stacking their rifles to one side and inviting our students to join them in games, children's games—playing ring-around-a-rosy and blindman's buff. There was no fighting, no looting, no mistreatment of women. It was the best disciplined army that China had ever seen. We looked at the walls and saw notices, reading "We guarantee freedom of religion." . . . Another notice I was very happy to see: "Protect the property of the foreigner." People came in from the village, and said, "We have never seen soldiers like this before in our lives. They even sweep up the streets of the village for us at night."

Here was action propaganda of the most effective sort.

The narrator goes on at once to explain that this approach, which he calls "missionary," was "far more dangerous" than truculent behavior such as had been anticipated, because it was so disarming. This is not to say that the discipline observed and the consideration for personal rights that was shown was merely a matter of shrewdness. The point is that the degree of humaneness and friendliness authorized or permitted under the Communist regime was determined first and last by the anticipated effect on the fortunes of the revolution.

A report on the Guatemala struggle over Communism declares that "Communism used the Catholic religion as its first wedge to gain entrance into the heart of the peasant." The propaganda line was that Communist doctrine was the "doctrine of Leo XIII."

An informing report from Argentina says, "The Communist tactic and strategy is to appeal to the ethical teachings of Jesus, and to compare the approach of the social workers of the Christian Church in many fields of the world as the true Communist approach."

A nationally known American editor wrote me: "I had the opportunity to interview American soldiers just after they had been released from Communist prison camps. It was interesting, in talking to them, to discover that the attempt to win them over to Communism had been through the use of the Christian ethic." He quotes one returnee who said the Communists were not against Christianity. He reported: "They even encouraged us to Christian worship. They said that Communism was what happened when you applied the idea of Jesus to economics."

One may confidently say that in many instances Communists, in their effort to be all things to all men, have made the most of the social-ethical elements in Christianity—and in other high religions—as a means of convincing those outside their fold that commitment to ethical ends and social betterment is a reason for rather than against alignment with Communism. Yet there is evidence that the cleavage between biblical faith, on the one hand, and Communist "scientism" and class war, on the other, has led to strong emphasis on their incompatibility. The variety of approach is very wide. An exceptionally shrewd observer, with varied experience in encounter with Communism writes:

I should like to say that so far as I have observed the Communists have not made a concerted campaign to win over Christians. On the contrary, I had a feeling that they tended to distrust active Christians. Nor do I feel that the Communist party had what I would call an "evangelistic" approach. No one ever approached me, directly or indirectly, in an effort to convert me to Communism, and it is my impression that, particularly in the Soviet Union, the stress was entirely on the self-sacrifice that was expected of Communist party members.

From other sources we have been assured that evangelism is a major Communist weapon. For example,

there was a planned systematic attempt to win converts to Communism among Christians. The Communist Youth Corps on the Yenching Campus, 1949, systematically singled out Christian students for pressure, sometimes assigning Communist students in relays to wear down opposition thinking. One of the leaders of the Student Christian Association, the son of a minister, was very early converted in this manner. The methods used were a combination of reasoned approach, flattery, and later, veiled intimidation, but stressing more than any other one thing an appeal to Chinese patriotism.

Another letter, reporting on South China, says the Communists "make definite attempts to win leaders, educated leaders, and in Fukien Province many of the leaders were Christians. They made very specific and systematic attempts, and succeeded, in trying to win students in Christian high schools—middle schools —and also in the large Amoy University which was a government school. This latter was riddled with them, and all were aware of it, before Fukien Province became theirs completely." The writer later observed the same pattern in Iraq.

This missionary approach may at times have a coarse and sinister aspect. A missionary in the Far East sends this significant comment:

> Every Communist was on fire with zeal to win converts. Their method was through disillusionment and bribes, followed by threats, frustration, and force. Constant conditioning and repetition break down a person's defiance until he begins to actually believe what he is told. He is especially susceptible to this conditioning because he is shut off from the rest of the world. He hears only the Communist lies, and has no way to find out the truth about current affairs with which to combat those lies. If one tended to acquiesce to the Communist appeal, the approach seemed to be more friendly and flattering, usually to the uneducated. . . . The inducement offered in our concentration camp was food—to hungry people. (No one who has never known the real meaning of hunger can appreciate the power of such a bribe.) There were also promises of high positions when the Communists would come into power over all the world.

It will be apparent to the reader, no doubt, that judgments of conflicting import are included here purposely in order to indicate how far from uniform the picture is. Also, the divergence shows the inner capacity and propensity of Communism to develop and maintain a multiform strategy in order to pursue a uniform and constant purpose. The more varied the pattern the more unvarying the ultimate purpose can be.

Use of Ritual

Related to this phase of our subject is a Communist practice, of unknown extent, by which an attempt is made to realize the ritualistic value of religion without any recognition of religious beliefs. The following account of a "socialist christening" or "youth dedication" in East Germany was made available to us from Y.M.C.A. sources:

For a number of years, the Socialist Unity Party (SED) in the Soviet Zone has been organizing ceremonies of a pseudo-religious character, called "Youth Dedication." Preparation for Youth Dedication takes place in so-called "youth classes" providing instruction in the spirit of historic dialectical materialism which is in complete opposition to the religious truths that Christian participants, especially members of confirmation classes, are taught by Church and family—in opposition also, of course, to science that is independent of party doctrines. Therefore, the churches have declared that participation in Youth Dedication is incompatible with Communion and Confirmation. On the other hand, State and Party maintain that Youth Dedication does not interfere with religious liberty and liberty of conscience as guaranteed in the Constitution of the "German Democratic Republic"; also, it was pointed out in the beginning that participation in youth classes and youth dedication was voluntary. However, from year to year the materialistic and pseudo-religious character of this practice has become increasingly evident, and participation has been enforced by growing pressure on parents and children. Without any hesitation, the incompatibility of the dogma, preached in youth classes, with Christian religion is emphasized today. . . .

A "name-giving dedication" took place on Christmas Day 1957 at Altenburg, Thuringia; three children were received into the "socialist community." The "dedication" ceremony had been planned and prepared by the "Committee for Name-Giving": in the Registrar's Office a special room, similar to the vestry of a church, had been set aside. Even a harmonium was there. The table of the registrar was decorated with flowering plants and lighted with candles. . . .

The ceremony was opened with the "Largo" by Handel. Then the Registrar held a speech in which he said: . . .

. . . "This Socialist Name-Giving is an affirmation of allegiance to our workers' and farmers' state, the first Socialist German state. You have now become part of those who share in the struggle for peace, Socialism and Progress. . . .

"You, dear parents and relatives, will have to see to it that from early childhood these children are brought up to become positively socialist persons. These children will not only experience the socialist order of society, but also Communism. We will have to be those who shape this society, who continue Lenin's work. Our state, which bestows upon our children all its love and care, will help you in this regard. They will be able to develop according to their own talents. . . ."

Communist Fronts

One pattern which in its very nature the Communists have found to be widely applicable is the "front" type of organization. Two designations have acquired currency—"Communist front" and "united front." Both engage attention here chiefly as applicable to the American situation. The two are quite different in their rationale and in their public impact, yet very similar in strategic import and utility. The Communist front is, typically, contrived by Communists who try to keep in the background and so conceal the origin of the project, whatever it may be. The ostensible immediate purpose—and commonly a genuine one, so far as it goes—is one that promises potentially wide support entirely without reference to ideology, but its success is largely dependent on concealment of the fact that it sprang from Communist initiative and gets its main drive from that source. A good example of the united front was the American League Against War and Fascism—later, the American League for Peace and Freedom—which was very active during World War II. Such an organization appeals to a sufficiently large section of the public and creates, or responds to, a sufficient degree of urgency that participation in it by Communists is accepted as plausible and even desirable. In other words it is a united front within the limits of its major declared purpose.

The Communist front has an essentially conspiratorial character because a full and frank statement of its ulterior purpose is bound to result in many defections on the part of people who feel that they have been taken in. The united front, arising out of some great emergency or threat of disaster, has a longer expectation of life. Obviously, World War II was a gigantic experiment in creating and maintaining a united front. It seems clear that the multiplication of front organizations which gave rise to a vast hysteria in this country—as well as a wholesome but controlled concern among the more sober-minded—was an inevitable result of the war and its diplomatic aftermath. The crest of this skillfully organized activity seems to have long since passed, though many people are still victims of the mentality resulting from it.

I confess to a measure of inner conflict here. As one who felt deep resentment and a sense of moral outrage over hidden front activities of the sort above described, I have nevertheless been made uncomfortable by the disparity between the degree of con- cerned involvement manifested by Communists and their open sympathizers over cases of patent social injustice and that of which recognized Christian leaders give evidence. When the famous Scottsboro case—involving several Negro youths who were tried for alleged rape of a white woman—was attracting wide attention there was good reason to believe that it became a *cause célèbre* chiefly because of all-out championship of the defense by the Communist party. To many of us this seemed like exploitation, with possible dire consequences for the boys. I made a point of this when discussing the case with a national Communist leader. His quick response was, "If we had not taken up their case those boys would have been executed long ago." Whatever answer was in order, it did not come to mind.

The study by Ralph Lord Roy, cited earlier, sums up concisely the nature and extent of the Communist fronts:

During critical periods, new fronts sprang up almost daily. There were fronts for young and old; for mothers, wives and daughters; for veterans and the jobless; for Jews, Negroes, Poles, Italians; for American-born and foreign-born. They were never called fronts, as was occasionally true when the concept was originally put into practice. Now they were councils, committees, conferences, congresses, clubs, forums, foundations, federations, societies, and associations. There were also schools, dramatic groups, information centers, even summer camps for "democratic living." These fronts were established to defend, to free, to uphold, to win, to secure, to aid, to battle, to resist, to fight, to struggle. They wanted peace, justice, democracy, the Bill of Rights. They did not want war, injustice, white supremacy, unemployment, higher rents, rising food costs, police brutality, inadequate housing, censorship, militarism, monopolies.[3]

[3] *Op. cit.,* p. 191.

Fellow Travelership

It is in the fellow-traveler category that we find most of the Communist-inspired activities on the part of intellectuals—educators, ministers, writers, and so forth—which, in the United States, have occasioned charges of subversion or lesser mischief. That is to say, among us it is not the Communists themselves, but persons who occupy positions of leadership in civic affairs, education, and religion who are the chief cause of alarm and the chief targets of criticism. That this should be the case was probably inevitable in view of the mixture of social and antisocial elements which our study has brought into sharp relief. In encounters with Communism persons who are strongly opposed to it on religious and philosophical grounds are nevertheless challenged by the social concerns embodied in Communist party programs. Here the real confrontation is not between Communism and democracy or between Communism and Christianity. It is between anti-Communists, alarmed and so militant, who condemn the system as totally diabolic and persons so concerned for democracy and human betterment as to believe it morally wrong to withhold support from some cause they approve solely because it has Communist support.

It must be recalled at once, of course, that there are also Christians, few but conspicuous and not without influence, who have convinced themselves that Communism is, on balance, in harmony with Christianity and, indeed, that it affords the best available means of implementing Christian social ethics in the economic sphere. Most of us find such a judgment incomprehensible and mischievous, but there it is. The files of the present study illustrate this amply. Some of the relevant material was included in Chapter III. A striking feature of our inquiry has been the extent to which Christian leaders who have long been close observers of political developments in Europe and Asia—leaders who never became involved as fellow travelers—have showed concern over what they regard as the vulnerablity of the Western world to the moral attack aimed at us by Communists. The churches are, of course, involved in this because, as our theologians continually remind us, the existential church is always conditioned by the culture. Since the cutting edge of the Communist critique is applied to social and economic conditions and to the frustration of aspirations to political independence on the part of less privileged peoples, enemies of the West find it easy to make their indictment in ethical terms.

By the same token Christians who are responsive to the social imperatives of Christian ethics may feel an obligation to "witness" to particular Communist achievements. An extreme example is that of the missionary in China, serving on the staff of a Christian university, who wrote to an American minister: "Now we are having a thrilling experience of reorganizing every phase of our university life, and of Chinese society. It is the most profoundly religious Christian experience I have ever been through. I absolutely believe this to be the most comprehensive renaissance the human spirit has ever experienced; and the most dynamic change in human history. God is working alongside of these Communists."

Manifestly, then, fellow travelership is not monolithic. Some of those who play that role are apparently confused. Some become caught in a conspiratorial web and behave disingenuously when their relationship is publicly exposed, but some, however mistaken we judge them to be, are transparently honest and have the courage of their radical convictions. We are including them all in this discussion of Communist methods of winning support because fellow travelers are obviously a great asset of the Communist movement and must be reckoned with as such. They constitute, in some sense, an auxiliary Communist apparatus, in spite of the fact that comprised in the fellow traveler group are men and women of very diverse political and social outlooks, intentions, and affiliations. This is not to be wondered at, since in the mind of the public at large "fellow traveler" is an omnibus term including all who have a conspicuous propensity for doing and saying things that are likely to give aid and comfort to the enemy. In time of great tension and general apprehensiveness few of us are disposed to make fine distinctions among people who are deemed alike with respect to the one paramount matter: Increasing a common danger.

The loyal American citizen who is devoted to democratic

principles and who has a passion for civil liberty and for the abolition of war is more than likely to incur suspicion on the part of those who believe that destruction of the Communist menace should take precedence over all other objectives. It is quite patent that some undoubtedly sincere and dedicated Christians, conspicuously exemplary in character, have supplied fuel for the fire of fanatical anti-Communism. This has created a serious problem for churches and church agencies—not in numerical terms, but because of the gravity of the issues raised, the ramifications of resulting controversy, and the effect on policy making and relations with the public. Moreover, this following of the Communist line, though wholly on the responsibility of the individual concerned—not as a result of external control or pressure—amounted to a taking over—presumably unwittingly in some cases—of the Communist principle of "centralism" and forsaking the authentically democratic policy that the agency professed to carry out. Admittedly a difficult question arises here, for by and large, the voluntary organizations and agencies, religious and secular, that thrive in our culture seek to protect individual freedom—in pulpit, press, classroom, and the functioning of organization executives—and are reluctant to tie the hands of those to whom leadership has been entrusted. Indeed, one reason for the sharp attacks on some of our agencies as "red" or "pink" is this tendency to preserve freedom of individual "witness" and the consequent refusal to repudiate or remove from their positions persons who have lost their following but who are believed to be devoted and sincere. In Protestant churches there is a weighty tradition to the effect that personal freedom is so great a treasure as to warrant some risk for its preservation. It is still a fair question whether the deliberate noninterference by church authorities with the freedom of leaders who had become targets of criticism for Communist leanings was not sometimes justified as resistance to reactionary hysteria. Such a liberal policy is certainly in order where anti-Communism has gone to the length of stigmatizing activities or utterances that were entirely consistent with Christian faith and practice, solely because some Communist group or official organ was advocating the same things. The Communist line should not be defined by particular items of policy, but by the total drive of the Communist apparatus. There could be no more abject surrender to the Communists than to follow the line in reverse—shaping policy by opposing everything the Communists are advocating.

The other side of this picture, however, also has a grievous aspect. It can be best portrayed, perhaps by a reference to the privately recorded experience of an able and highly regarded American churchman who has a liberal social outlook. He writes concerning the ways in which radical leadership, presumably quite conscientious but patently following the Communist line, was able to establish and buttress itself in Christian organizations. It has sometimes seemed that the intensity of anti-Communist propaganda, often undiscriminating, has defeated its own ends by arousing sympathy, sometimes equally undiscriminating, which erects a defense for persons who are attacked—particularly where personal freedom seems to be jeopardized. Priceless possessions like freedom of the pulpit, of teaching, and of the press —and we must add, of the organization executive—have been repeatedly stretched beyond all reasonable bounds. The correspondent referred to writes concerning his experiences in this kind of situation. "Arrangements," he says, were skillfully made "for the muffling of criticism, for the rallying of 'liberal opinion' against those who were no redbaiters, but were trying to clean house before matters reached the stage of becoming a public scandal. This was as successful as anything which the Communists and fellow travelers did in my experience." In one case, where actual infiltration of a student organization had been effected, funds improperly diverted, and records falsified, charges were preferred and an investigation ordered—all to no avail. He says:

Those of us who made the charges and thought that we had proved them to the hilt were astonished to find ourselves called redbaiters, and to find that our "liberal" friends simply would not accept the evidence even when they should have had sense enough to know that the people who were defining the problem were not redbaiters in any sense, had themselves been called Communist many times by the more ignorant, and were trying, if anything, to prevent a public scandal from developing."

When all has been said, however, about fellow travelership, the fact remains that to one person a fellow traveler may appear a well-intentioned but uncritical enthusiast while another person may regard him as a dangerous conspirator.

In the following section we shall take a closer look at what religion has at stake in the Communist revolution.

5
COMMUNISM AND RELIGION

In earlier sections of this report we have considered many aspects of the encounter between Christianity and Communism —more broadly, between Communism and all traditional religion. We must now examine further the nature of the conflict, why it is so charged with ambiguities and apparent contradictions, and what the prospects are for effective missionary effort and personal spiritual influence in those regions where Communism is a dominant force. Of first importance in such inquiry is of course the outlook for indigenous movements, so promisingly represented in recent years by the younger churches. Vital cultural contact is basic to institution building. My own observations in "mission lands" have inspired respect for the cultural receptivity exhibited by many of the present generation of missionary leaders who have learned that American or British Christianity is not "for export" in stereotyped fashion, but that continual change in pattern and presuppositions is inevitable and desirable. Is such an observation relevant to the present inquiry?

This is not to suggest that every nation or geographic region can be an independent arbiter of what Christianity means, but rather that a dynamic conception of the Christian faith will take account of cultural and historical factors peculiar to an ethnic or a national group. Is not this implicit in the idea of ecumenicity? Diversity may be as significant as unity.

A Deceptive Resemblance

We must always remember that our basic problem in dealing with Communism at the spiritual level is not peculiar to the

Christian Church, but concerns religion in general. Communism has no unique quarrel with Christianity per se, except that its major encounter with religion in the Soviet Union has been with particular forms of Christianity—Eastern Orthodoxy, Roman Catholicism, and certain Protestant denominations. There is no important difference as far as the Soviet government is concerned between Christianity and Judaism or between either of them and Islam. Communism has clashed with them all. To the extent that the Jewish community has a special grievance against the Soviet government—and there is much evidence to support it —the reasons are primarily cultural and political, not religious. The antagonism to religion as such rests chiefly on practical considerations. Religion is considered a sort of moral anesthetic, deadening one's concern for what has to be done in the here and now and diverting attention to otherworldly hopes and expectations. Thus religion is charged with breeding moral irresponsibility. Moreover, antitheistic teaching and crusading is assumed to be necessary, especially with the young, in order to establish a firm and durable commitment to the Communist philosophy—historical, dialectical materialism.

It would go without saying that the attitude of official Communism toward religion in general is negative. Nevertheless the problem with which Communism confronts Christianity arises, in large part, because of a certain correspondence between Christianity and Communism in terms of avowed ethical and social ends. Thus Communism has its own eschatology—a veritable apocalyptic vision of a secular paradise in which there will be no economic strife. It has a secular version of what has long been a major concern of Christianity, namely, the transformation of character; this was to Paul "a new creation," it is in Russia, the "new Soviet man." It is a striking fact that the Communist movement has undertaken to achieve something corresponding to the Christian concept of being "born again" and, concomitantly, a regeneration of society, which Christianity also contemplates but in a different pattern. Moreover, in many instances the actual concrete programs and planned activities of Communist parties and governments include elements that can claim high sanction from a Christian viewpoint.

In a sense, then, Communism's threat to Christianity is largely due to a deceptive resemblance between them. This is what theologians mean when they refer to the "demonic" aspect of Communism—a quality that has some intrinsic merit which, however, is neutralized or perverted by the evil ends that it is made to serve or the good ends which it serves to obscure. A perceptive Catholic writer has recently put it this way, "What is demonic in Communism is that it takes a partial truth and seeks to make it the whole."

The verdict of classical Christianity upon the ethical philosophy of Communism has been tersely stated by Joseph L. Hromádka, a Czech theologian who has been severely criticized by many church leaders as partial to the Communist movement—a fact which gives special significance to his statement. "We do not believe," he said, "in any possibility of an ideological synthesis of Communism and Christian faith. Such a synthesis is impossible. They find themselves on a different level." [1] Concerning the "goal of the Communist social, economic, and political planning: *a classless society,*" Hromádka said:

A Christian has no objection to this kind of social democracy. In many ways he agrees that a political democracy is not sufficient for securing human freedom and dignity. His criticism is directed against the idea that this society has a redeeming power capable of solving all human moral, economic, political, and international problems. . . . A Christian knows that even a classless society will be a society of sinners, of selfish, corruptible men, and that such a society will badly need the message of the divine grace, forgiveness, redemption, and self-denying love.[2]

I have reproduced Hromádka's statement precisely because he is a controversial figure often criticized as pro-Communist. His political orientation makes his theological statement more impressive.

---

[1] From *Theology Between Yesterday and Tomorrow* by Joseph L. Hromádka. Copyright 1957, W. L. Jenkins. The Westminster Press. By permission.

[2] *Ibid.,* pp. 85-86.

A "Christian Heresy"?

This ambivalence of Communism, when looked at from a biblical standpoint, is the reason why some theologians have called it a "Christian heresy." Philosophically, it is, of course, an Hegelian heresy, forcing Hegel's rational "dialectic" of ideas into a rigid materialistic mold. Marx borrowed from Hegel the dialectic concept, in the sense of historically inevitable encounter between opposites—"thesis" and "antithesis"—resulting in a new "synthesis." Polar opposites are conceived as, in fact, interpenetrating and giving rise to something essentially novel. As Marx himself said, however, he turned Hegel's dialectic upside down from Hegel's point of view, right side up from his own. Thus the Marxist philosophy is essentially materialistic. Nevertheless, such eminent Christian scholars as the late Archbishop William Temple and the Roman Catholic philosopher Jacques Maritain have considered "heresy" an apt term in this context.[3]

For our purposes it is sufficient to note that a movement which embodies such ideas and concerns as those above referred to makes some comparison with Christianity unavoidable in any serious study of its impact on personal loyalties and on the course of human affairs. This is particularly true when it becomes apparent that Christians in considerable numbers have felt the pull of this startlingly dynamic secular movement.

Conversely, Christianity's exaltation of human brotherhood and equality has led idealistic devotees of Communism to call Christianity "a Communist heresy." This is doubtless partly because the many experiments in communal living which the early Christian community inspired, beginning with the very small one recorded in the Acts of the Apostles, have received no more than token support from Christians. Of more serious import, however, is the fact that the vast spread of institutional Christianity has in no small measure obscured the ethos of the early Church, with its emphasis on community, fellowship, and sharing.

I must record here that some scholarly persons to whom a preliminary précis of this book was submitted for criticism found these last observations rather wild and repellent. However, the

[3] See Cuninggim, *op. cit.*, pp. 75 ff.

volume referred to above which embodied the results of the earlier phase of our study includes an entire chapter devoted to this notion of Christianity as a Communist heresy, indicating a consensus of a group of scholars that it requires serious attention, regardless of how the idea may be evaluated.[4] The very fact that it has ever been so characterized is revealing as to the nature of the Communist-Christian encounter. Such a proposition is of course judgmental rather than factual, since it is not susceptible of proof. Viewed in this light, I am disposed to regard the contention that Christianity is a Communist heresy as the legitimate converse from the Communist point of view of the contention that Communism is a Christian heresy from the Christian standpoint.

This matter is by no means trivial. Some of the expositors of Marxism who have given it classic expression have evidenced great interest in the history of Christianity. Feuerbach and Kautsky are examples that come readily to mind. The socialist movement in both its democratic and its Communist forms—which are in sharp contrast to each other philosophically and ethically—has been influenced by Christian social militancy on behalf of the depressed and the exploited. It is not to be supposed that the words of the Magnificat—the "storm-song of democracy"—were lost on the apostles of the social revolution: "He hath shewed strength with his arm; he hath scattered the proud in the imagination of their hearts. He hath put down the mighty from their seats, and exalted them of low degree. He hath filled the hungry with good things; and the rich he hath sent empty away." (Luke 1:51-53.) Initially, Christianity was not without a measure of class consciousness, albeit not of the Communist stripe. The significance of these aphorisms about heresy comes down to this: The Christian critique of Communism finds it, in actuality, a perversion of ideals and purposes which it theoretically embodies; while the Communist critique of Christianity in its visible, institutional forms, finds it guilty of apostasy from its original commitment to the cause of the poor and the disinherited.

[4] *Ibid.*, pp. 97-118.

While the remarks that follow may seem to some readers gratuitous in such a book as this, I am constrained to introduce them in this discussion in the interest of a clearer understanding of the way Communists think and the way their system operates. It is doubtless inevitable that systems which are arrayed against each other and are mutually regarded as threats should give rise to "images" which are only in part true.

A Communist Ethic?

For example, it is commonly said that there is no Communist ethic except the ethic of force; that war is, in the Communist philosophy, necessarily the final arbiter between the classes. Now the truth in this charge must be set over against the universal tendency among even the most civilized nations to subordinate ethical considerations to political or military necessity in time of national emergency and crisis. No nation is willing to renounce war unconditionally, and once war has broken out traditional ethics are virtually suspended. The obligation to tell the truth is completely neutralized by the requirements of military intelligence. Espionage, though without sanction in law, is carried on as a practical necessity. No matter how eloquently we contend in peacetime that "the end does not justify the means," in war the contrary is assumed. Property rights, ordinarily held inviolable among democratic peoples, get short shrift when enemy property is dealt with.

Until recent years it has been widely assumed that even war could be carried on in relatively civilized fashion—that there are certain destructive measures which no government with a sense of moral responsibility would use—but it is probably safe to say that since August, 1945, a considerable part of the American people have carried a sense of guilt for having initiated the use of a lethal weapon, the possibility of whose invention had up to that time scarcely been imagined. These are chastening thoughts, and in the present context they are exceedingly important, for once the Marxist theory concerning the perpetual hostility of economic classes and the inevitability of class war is accepted, it easily follows in Communist thinking that since the one great

103

war that really matters, the class war, is always in progress, the crudest and most immoral of devices acquire sanction just as the atomic bomb did sixteen years ago. "Necessity is the mother of invention" is an aphorism that seems to apply almost without exception to the thinking and behavior of a nation that feels itself to be under a threat of great disaster. Communist thinking is crudely parallel.

This is said not to extenuate a false political and economic theory or the philosophy underlying it, but rather to throw light on human motivation under the pressure of circumstance. In a moral encounter between nations, classes, parties, or institutions a primary requirement is to understand why things that seem patently reprehensible are sanctioned by intelligent human beings.

Communist Philosophy

Moreover, it is somewhat surprising that the case against Communism is so often made to rest on the charge of "false philosophy." That is to say, the denial of transcendent, objective moral law and of ultimate principles that have universal validity is often interpreted as a complete negation of morality, and hence as intolerable. I mention this here for one purpose only, namely, to indicate that such an indictment of Communist philosophy would be fatal also if directed against a very extensive school of philosophy which is quite respectable in the West. It is the philosophy of naturalism, with its evolutionary conception of morality. It can hardly be denied that many American scholars who are held in high repute and whose character is exemplary hold to a naturalistic philosophy which when put forward under the aegis of Communism provokes severe condemnation and is even held to be ground for punitive action. Toleration has its limits, to be sure, but logic has its requirements. John C. Bennett has said, Communism in itself is "no more atheistic than any naturalistic philosophy that accepts the experienced world of nature and history as self-sufficient." It would probably be nearer the truth, he thinks, to regard dialectical materialism as "a form of monistic naturalism." [5] One cannot consistently make Bolshevik metaphysics ground for a crusade against Communism while remaining complacent about theological "heresy" among American educators.

"Other Worldliness" a Target

One could pursue this line at some length, applying it to Marx's economic determinism, comparing the latter with Calvinist theology, and making other comparisons which indicate no necessary correspondence between metaphysical assumptions and moral capacity. Even in the matter of religion evidence is not wanting that the systematic warfare waged by Communism against religion rests in no small part on the assumption that preoccupation with religious ultimates is bound to deaden concern for human problems as they are confronted in this present world. A striking passage in an official document prepared for the direction of "atheistic education" in the Soviet Union bases the "exposure" of religion on this ground. It warns against the danger of distorting the real purpose of antireligious education and slipping into

a campaign against the church and its ministers, which would be wrong. In the first place, we must not forget that religion may exist without the church and its ministers, without its reactionary nature being thereby in the least diminished; and in the second place, there have been and still are cases in which individual religious organizations, and still more, individual members of the clergy, have played and still play in our time a relatively progressive role. Such for example was the role of many monasteries in the early Middle Ages, in the spreading of literacy, the role of the priest Huss in the struggle for the national independence of Bohemia; such moreover was the role in the second World War of many representatives of the clergy of our own and of other lands, of the anti-Hitlerite coalition, who came out vigorously against those modern cannibals, contributed funds for the war against Germany and

[5] *Christianity and Communism Today* (rev. ed.) ; New York: Association Press, 1960, pp. 34, 35.

her allies, and who now come out in defence of peace throughout the world, against the forces of aggression.[6]

To repeat, a major reason given for opposing religion is that it promotes otherworldliness and indifference to the problems of this life. This reflects, of course, a thoroughly negative attitude toward religion and religious institutions, but not necessarily the built-in hostility to religious ideals as such which is commonly assumed.

On the other hand, it is patent that Communism despises the Christian doctrine that the meek shall inherit the earth. Here again, however, there is dismal evidence that this maxim is in effect repudiated by a substantial portion of our own people.

The point I am seeking to make is that we are constantly weakening our case against Communism by using arguments that are less than convincing to great numbers of people in many nations whom we desperately need to convince.

Let us be wholly clear as to the reasons for the effort to find the points at which Christian teaching and Communist philosophy appear to penetrate each other. This book is no attempt to make the repugnant features of Communism any less detestable. The essential drive of Communism is inimical to all high religion. In many respects it remains true that Communism stands for precisely what biblical religion abhors. The point is that we must come to terms with the fact that Communism is winning adherents and sympathizers among the ranks of those who believe themselves to be standing in the best Western tradition. Why is this? And what does it imply for a valid strategy vis-à-vis the Communist revolution?

Some confusion attends the familiar Marxist dictum, "Religion . . . is the opium of the people"—used with slightly variant wording. It has sometimes been attributed to Charles Kingsley. Indeed, one of our correspondents said he wished "Kingsley *had* said it," because it characterizes a form of religion,

[6] E. I. Petrousky, "Atheistic Education in the School." Translated from the Russian by Stephen Schmidt, S.J., and published in *Christ to the World*, Rome, 1956-57, I, 138-53; II, 102-13. The above quotation was taken from a reprint, "Statement of Principles and Policy on Atheistic Education in Soviet Russia," issued by John A. Hardon, S.J., West Baden College, West Baden Spring, Ind., 1958, p. 19.

or religiosity, which is not too far from Marx's generalization. In any case it is simple truth that contemporary critics of religion—particularly the type not uncommonly found in the currently increasing religious population of America—have seen much to condemn in what Marx apparently had in mind.[7] This kind of religion was very familiar in Jesus' day and he characterized it as the "mint and anise and cummin" type of religion.

The all-important point here is that Christian social criticism, especially in social-gospel literature, has always made much of the excessive individualism of the church—some would say, especially of the Protestant churches—and the consequent failure to develop a vigorous social criticism of the structure of society itself. The latter has always been the essence of the social-gospel movement, and I believe it is still dominant in the prophetic leadership of Christianity in the United States.

Soviet Policy Concerning Religion

As in virtually all aspects of Communist theory and practice, there are ambiguities and contradictions in policy concerning religion. In Russia, for example, it was early discovered that to undertake a wholesale suppression of religion was ill-advised, since the government had its hands full of this-worldly problems without seeking to change deep-seated beliefs and habits of worship. (A high official of the Russian Communist party once told me as much.) A compromise was indicated: Proclaiming freedom of worship, while carrying on a vigorous atheistic—or more precisely, antitheistic—educational program. In this way the stage was set for the rearing of Communists—"professional unbelievers"—while the stigma of religious persecution was, at least formally, avoided. It is a matter of common remark that the prime target of Communist ideological indoctrination is the youth of the country. The Communism in the Soviet Union obviously does not

[7] Illuminating, though not especially important, is the similar confusion about the words often attributed to Marx: "Thank God I'm no Marxist." More credible is the alternative version, according to which Marx was listening to a lecture in Paris purporting to be an exposition of his philosophy, and exclaimed in disgust, "Je ne suis pas Marxist!" The common version ascribes to Marx an intellectual humility that is certainly not Marxist.

regard such education as a recruitment device, for the party is a relatively small, disciplined group that in Communist theory constitutes an elite which is an indispensable instrument of the revolution. The ardor with which the materialist philosophy is propagated presumably signifies a paramount concern, as far as the masses are involved, for developing a national mentality of acceptance, of followership—a quality that religion does not find congenial. Hence the entire drive of Soviet education must be consistent with the official philosophy, and organized religion must be policed, so to speak, but not to the point of palpably robbing the people of their faith.

Such a policy is bound to exhibit ambiguities, as when Soviet statesmen insist that the people's religious beliefs must be respected, while Communist functionaries are complaining about the icons and religious ceremonials that persist in spite of exhortation or ridicule. Then, too, it is impossible to define any particular policy of a totalitarian regime by reference to single pronouncements or edicts, for in order to maintain comparative docility the rulers must alternately tighten and loosen the controls as the mood of the public requires.

It should be said also that what the Communists find most objectionable in religion is the "supernatural" emphasis. They are doubtless unaware that this is a controversial point among theologians in the non-Communist world. One is a bit startled, however, by the featuring of sacred Christian art in an official Soviet publication. For example, the September, 1960, issue of *USSR* had an article on the work of Andrei Rublyov, with reproductions in rich color and descriptions that were reverential in tone, as a few sentences and phrases will evidence:

The Savior is painted with Russian features, his gaze kindly and calm, but judging. This is the wise, understanding and loving guardian the Russian people were hoping for in this turbulent period of Tatar invasions and feudal rule.

The face of the Apostle Paul embodies the resolution and wisdom of the philosopher. . . .

The Archangel Michael. . . . In the ethereal blues, golds and rose-reds of the icon Rublyov seems to have painted the reflection of the apostle's radiant inner world.

Concerning a white-stone cathedral: "Unfortunately the frescoes have not survived, but we do have the iconostasis. . . . Symbolized is the Last Supper."

Contemplation of this exhibit brought to my mind the report published in 1957 of a psychological study of a group of Russian *émigrés*, a "summary" of which follows:

The responses of 165 postwar Soviet emigres to three propaganda passages involving religious themes were examined for gross and subtle indices of religiosity by four Russians with intimate knowledge of the Soviet scene and with religious convictions ranging from highly positive to indifferent. Their judgments, which were in close agreement, pointed to a wide prevalence of religious sentiment among contemporary Soviet youth of varying degree and nature. This conclusion was illuminated and reinforced by historical analysis and the analysis of probable past and present psychological factors, as well as by converging evidence derived from the data of interviews, correspondence, and the Soviet and Russian emigre press. The over-all conclusion drawn is that religious sentiment is not only widespread among the Soviet younger generation, but on the increase.[*]

Is "sentiment" perhaps more significant in this context than formal statements of belief?

It is a mistake, however, and a very common one in the West, to interpret the secularism of the Marxist-Leninist philosophy in wholly negative terms with respect to belief. Communism does not make a religion of its atheism; no one can build a religion, even a secular one, on a negation. It might almost be said that the devoted apostle of Communism seeks to invoke a convincing cosmic sanction against all the traditional faiths because he regards them as wrong and mischievous. There is more than a hint of this in the comments of missionaries who lament the inadequate and often ineffectual outward thrust of Western Christianity.

The melancholy paradox involved in all this was pointed up

[*] Ivan D. London and Nikolai P. Poltoratzky, "Contemporary Religious Sentiment in the Soviet Union," *Psychological Reports* (1957), Monograph Supplement 3, p. 128. Southern Universities Press, Box 11, Grand Forks, N. D. Used by permission.

in the report of the American Quaker delegation to Russia a few years ago. In a section on the nature of freedom in the report these Quakers said:

It is a commonplace of Christian theological writing that man finds true freedom only in submission to the will of God. In the same way Soviet man is told that he can find true freedom only by understanding the laws of nature as revealed through Marxism-Leninism and by shaping his life according to them. Since the Communist party by definition is the supreme authority on the Marxist faith, the individual is expected to look to the party for guidance in all areas of life. . . . "Each one of us writes according to the dictates of his own heart, and our hearts belong to the party and our people whom we serve with our art." Freedom is to be found by handing over one's heart—and one's conscience—to the party, which by definition represents the real interests of the people.[9]

Engels, following Hegel, defined freedom as "the recognition of necessity."

What is the actual status of the churches in the Soviet Union? A few generalizations may be made with a good deal of confidence.

The official attitude of the Soviet Government toward religion has never changed since the October Revolution, except as opposition was greatly reduced during World War II. The effort to eliminate religion by means of propaganda and restrictive measures has been continuous ever since the revolution.

Toward the end of the 1920's it looked as though organized church life in Russia would be crushed out, but in 1927 Metropolitan Sergius obtained legal recognition for the church organization in exchange for a declaration of loyalty to the government. The general church council that he asked for at that time was not held until 1943. Sergius was then elected Patriarch, and the regime began which persists until today. Stalin apparently thought that the organized churches could be useful to him and the Soviet government.

A Commissariat for Orthodox Church Affairs, directly attached to the Council of Ministers, was established, and a second com-

[9] *Meeting the Russians.* American Quakers Visit the Soviet Union. A report prepared by the delegation (Philadelphia: American Friends Service Committee, 1956), p. 10.

missariat for all other religious bodies, including Protestants. Archbishop Boris stated that the purpose of these commissariats was "to see that legal relations between church and state are fulfilled."

The Commissar of Orthodox Church Affairs aids the church in many ways. He is liaison man between the church and the government. His representatives in other parts of the country serve in the same way between church and government organs. Before, the church was merely tolerated—now it has full recognition as an autonomous organization.

The party line with respect to the church changed at the beginning of the war. Stalin saw that to have the people behind the war effort he had to have the support of the church. As noted above, a patriarch was elected—an event of symbolic as well as practical importance. Seminaries were opened and a church publishing house was established. All antireligious propaganda stopped, and the "League of Militant Godless" was dissolved, never to reappear. Antireligious activity reappeared later, but not the "League of Militant Godless." During the war the church urged all Russians to fight in defense of the motherland, and large sums were collected for the war effort through church efforts.

The church continued to be useful to the government after the war, especially in foreign relations. For the first time in history a Russian patriarch visited patriarchs of the Near East, Antioch, and Jerusalem. Metropolitan Nicolai, "foreign minister" of the Russian Orthodox Church, took a leading part in the Moscow-supported World Council for the Defense of Peace. Here he often repeated Soviet slogans about peace and disarmament. As long as the church seems useful to the Soviet government it will presumably be permitted to carry on as at present.

Both Orthodox and Protestants say that they have no exact statistics as to their membership. The Orthodox Church includes in its membership baptized infants; the Protestants, only persons admitted in their teens or later. Protestant leaders estimate that they have 3,000,000 members in the U.S.S.R., a majority of whom are Baptists. An Orthodox spokesman has reported the Orthodox membership as between 40 and 50,000,000. Elderly people conspicuously predominate in attendance.

There is no conclusive indication of trends—whether or not the total membership is growing, though some observers report appreciable increase. One Orthodox priest in Moscow commented, "Our faithful are fewer in numbers than before the revolution, but higher in quality."

There are, however, many more candidates for admission to the eight theological seminaries and the two academies (university-grade schools) than these are able to accept. This is due partly to lack of space, partly to lack of competent teachers. The number actually graduating and taking orders is not sufficient to fill current vacancies. The large number of men who wish to enter seminaries is due in part to a real sense of calling to the church's service. Critics point out that seminary students have slightly better economic conditions than students in secular schools. A priest in a good parish may have a salary as good or better than that of an engineer, and although he lives under the Damoclean sword of the permanent Communist hatred of religion, his life is less restricted than that of most other Soviet citizens—no time-clock to punch, no quota to fulfill. This may also explain the attraction the priesthood has for some men.

The churches receive no direct financial subvention from the state, and they are permitted to manage their own financial affairs. In both Protestant and Orthodox churches the faithful give generously in the church collections. The idea of membership subscriptions and a planned budget is little known in Russia. The Orthodox have a large income from the manufacture and sale of candles, et cetera, of which they have a monopoly. Their prosperity is more evident than that of the Protestants because Orthodox churches are richly decorated, have elaborate vestments, and so forth. The Baptists apparently have no financial difficulties, however. Indeed, it is reliably reported that the clergy of both Orthodox and Protestant churches are showing signs of real affluence. This state of affairs reflects the high level of employment and the relative scarcity of consumers' goods. A member of a church delegation to Russia reported: "In major cities the priests earn between 4,000 and 6,000 rubles a month—equal to the pay of a university lecturer." [10]

In the Soviet Union there is "encounter" between Christianity and Communism, but no "dialogue." Religion and the church are under continuous attack by the Communists.

Both Baptist and Orthodox Christians have said that their members discuss religious questions with fellow workmen at the workbench or in the mines, and that converts to Christianity are thus won. We have no indication as to how widespread this practice is.

There have been rare, but much publicized, cases of seminary students or other people publicly renouncing their religious faith in favor of materialism. This implied the acceptance of Marx's doctrines. There are rare cases—not at all publicized—of convinced Communists accepting Christianity. How far the young adults who are now accepting Christianity have ever been convinced Communists, it is impossible to say. Every phase of education in the U.S.S.R. is slanted toward atheism. Marxism is held up as the doctrine that will save mankind, hence for millions of Soviet citizens belief in Marxism is more natural and certainly better reasoned than Christianity is for most people of the West. In any case the number of "converts" in either direction is minimal.

The tendency to make the imperfections of the pre-Revolution Russian Church responsible for the hostility of the Soviet government to religion is only partly correct. In an insightful article, "The Orthodox Church in Soviet Russia," Paul B. Anderson, one of the best informed interpreters of contemporary Russia, wrote:

The weaknesses of the Church do not lie so much in the areas designated by Western Protestants—lack of specialized forms of religious education for youth, or the absence of parish activities. Rather they lie in the enforced insulation of the Church from the main streams of life and growth in the Soviet Union, and in the economic affluence of the higher clergy, which could both reduce their spiritual vitality and create a cleavage between them and their less favored flocks.

[10] *Time* (June 20, 1960), LXXV, No. 25, 68.

Characteristic of the first is the complete separation of religion from science, economic life and social studies. Professors and graduate students in theology write only on church history, usually patristics, or on doctrine. The first collection of five such dissertations was published in 1959. No religious works dealing with problems of modern society (except "peace") are published. In fact, the only regular publications of the Church are the official monthly journal of the Patriarchate, liturgical manuals and occasional collections of sermons by the top prelates of the Church. Even these publications can be distributed only within the Church; they cannot be sold in bookstores.[11]

Donald A. Lowrie, a high authority on religion in Russia to whom I am indebted for assistance in preparing this section, has written:

The fact is that after 44 years of intense efforts to crush religion in Russia, prosecuted by all the means available to the government of one of the most powerful and ruthless states in the world, religion does persist. Churches are full; somehow, many children receive religious upbringing; the Soviet press is constantly reporting the "alarming" spread of Christianity among young adults, and the church confirms the reports. Thousands of foreign visitors testify to the vitality of religion in Russia.[12]

Policy Different in U. S. Party

What will appear to be a digression is in order here. Because this book is being written primarily for American readers, it should be made clear that the Communist party in the United States has not followed the line laid down by the Soviet Union with respect to religion as it has in political matters. Whether or not Moscow considered this a deviation is immaterial to this discussion, but it is important to know that the party in this country has made a point of not warring on religion, systematically and on principle, and has, at least on occasion, sought friendly relations with a Christian body. The following excerpt from an appeal to Roman Catholics by Earl Browder, formerly head of

---

[11] *Foreign Affairs* (January, 1961), 39, no. 2, p. 310. Used by permission.
[12] Copyright 1961 Christian Century Foundation. Reprinted by permission from *The Christian Century*.

the Communist party in the United States, is revealing. Browder is no longer a Communist, but the document here quoted was published with a foreword by the National Committee of the party. It included:

Questions of religious belief have nothing to do with this problem. True, most Communists are not Catholics, although a growing number of the latter are joining our Party. But this is true of five-sixths of Americans, who are also non-Catholic. True, also, that most Communists profess no religion at all, and subscribe to a philosophy which finds no room for the supernatural element in solving social and economic problems, although in this matter there is no dogmatic obligation in Party membership and we have a growing number who retain their church affiliations. But this also is no cause for conflict between us, for Communists scrupulously respect all religious beliefs and avoid all offense against them, firmly upholding complete religious freedom and toleration. If our views contain error, according to the standards of Catholic doctrine, such error can differ only in degree from that of five-sixths of all Americans, who are also in error according to those doctrinal standards.

Questions of ethical standards are no foundation for any practical differences between Catholics and Communists. True, Catholics as a whole turn to the doctrines and dogmas of their Church for formulation and justification of ethical and moral standards, while Communists base their standards wholly on the needs of society, but in practical life, among the masses, it all comes to the same thing, justice, truth and fair dealing between man and man.

Questions of family and social morality furnish no practical division between Catholics and Communists, except in the same degree that they may divide Catholics and all non-Catholics, as in the question of the social permissibility of divorce, and so on. Contrary to much slander distributed by reactionary politicians in Catholic circles, the Communists are staunch upholders of the family. We consider sexual immorality, looseness and aberrations as the harmful product of bad social organization, and their increase in America today as largely products of the crisis of the capitalist system, of the demoralization among the upper classes which affects the masses by contagion, and we combat them as we combat all other harmful social manifestations.[13]

[13] *A Message to Catholics* (Workers Library Publishers, Inc., June, 1938), pp. 8-9. Used by permission.

This is one more evidence that the Communist movement is not monolithic. Its significance is that it represented Communism as not instrinsically hostile to Christianity, even in its most dogmatic form. At the same time the fact must be recognized that Communists are prepared to do anything to advance the cause.

Influence of Islam

It is frequently said that Islam may be counted on as a barrier to Communist expansion. There is a certain plausibility in this contention, which we may well note in the present context, though as a strategic consideration it hardly seems substantial. In his book *Islam in Modern History* W. Cantwell Smith has made a penetrating analysis of the typical Muslim community in religious and sociological terms.[14] Two major considerations emerge that are relevant here, though they might neutralize rather than reinforce one another in an encounter with Communism.

The first of these is the stress on community as a dynamic factor in Muslim society. Smith noted this "paramount position of the community" and continued: "Less thought has been devoted to the significance of Islamic history, which is that community in motion. It is well known that Muslim society has a remarkable solidarity, that the loyalty and cohesion of its members are intense. Many have recognized that the community is not only a social group but a religious body; that 'church and state' are one, to use the inappropriate language of the West." There is, at least on the surface, a suggestion here of susceptibility to the appeal of the "collectivity," which is central in Communism and which, as we have seen, has deep roots in Russian history. Concerning this concept of "a society in motion," the author said further: "In relation to this, the individual must not get out of step, must not turn deviationist; while group leadership is responsible for seeing that the whole venture knows and follows the right direction."

[14] (New York: New American Library of World Literature, 1959), pp. 26, 27, 28. Used by permission.

This has a familiar ring to the student of Communism. In the same context, however, Smith pointed out that the Muslim community is "the expression of a religious ideal" in a personal sense. "As a creed or theological system," he continued, "may be the expression in an intellectual form of a personal faith—as is often the case, particularly with Christians—so a social order and its activities are the expression in a practical form of a Muslim's personal faith. Just as to be a Communist involves being a member of the Party, so the religious conviction of a Muslim implies participation in the group." Obviously, this indicates a potential strong opposition. There are about 25,000,000 Muslims in the Soviet Union and about the same number in China. However, the amazing success of Communism in breaking through religious barriers to political conquest leaves little ground for confidence in an Islamic "dike" against its advance.

Impact on Religion in Red China

Turning now to mainland—Red—China, the other great Communist power where the regime goes virtually unchallenged, I am constrained to offer the reader excerpts from two memoranda which complement one another. One was furnished by a prominent and able Christian missionary leader; the other was written by a Chinese Christian scholar—the text translated into English by one of our most perceptive missionary executives.

The first document undertakes to interpret the impact of Communism on the Chinese Church. The excerpts that follow are especially pertinent to the present discussion:

Protestants are divided into two camps. There are those who refuse to come to terms with the Communist regime and accordingly have gone to prison or at least have ceased to operate. Others have made the necessary adjustments in order to satisfy the demands of the Communist regime, with the result that they represent a body of the Church which is operating above ground, preaching the gospel, and actively participating in the life and work of the nation.

It is easy for the Westerner to pass judgment on this latter group. Unless one has lived in an Asian country, or at least under a dictatorship, it little behooves him to be too critical of the decisions which those

117

Christians in China who presume to speak for the Church there are making. Our Christianity in the West is inherited; very few believers have paid any price for their faith. Christians in China, however, have adopted this faith generally from Westerners, and in many cases have paid a price for the new religion, a price often of persecution and of disqualification from the life of the community in which they were born. The Christian communities in the West generally are a majority of the total population; the Christian Church in China is a tiny minority, less than 1 per cent of the total. Much of Western culture is quasi-Christian; the culture of China is basically Confucian and Buddhist, and more recently Marxist. We in the West are free to do and say as we please; the Christians in China are not—they do not even have the freedom of silence. One of the tragedies of totalitarian rule is that all citizens are required by overt act or statement to demonstrate their loyalty to the regime. . . . The Christian faith in the West is assumed to be the religion of the people; in China the Christian faith is the religion of a tiny group of persons who are suspect because of prior connections with Westerners, who are today regarded as being the symbols of imperialism and capitalism, the two great enemies of the state.

The Chinese Christian community's difficulties did not begin with the Communist liberation of the country. . . . The Christians have been in trouble ever since the first missionaries of the West sought to establish a beachhead in China. The Manchu dynasty had closed the kingdom of China to the West. Trade restrictions which the Western powers suffered in seeking to deal with China led to the Opium War between Great Britain and China in 1840. . . . In imperial edicts issued in 1844 and 1846, edicts which grew out of negotiations between the Western powers and representatives of the Manchu dynasty and in which negotiations three Protestant missionaries played a part, Christians were granted the right to erect churches and the freedom of worship. Thus the Chinese have felt since the very beginning that Christianity was an exotic ideology and set of institutions imposed upon the nation by force. . . .

The Protestant Church suffered a great loss of membership immediately after the Chinese liberation which was completed about October, 1949. From that date until 1952 the membership of the churches dropped from approximately 1,000,000 to 600,000. Some of this was due to softness on the part of the Christians and possibly, also, to the disillusionment which they, as Christians, suffered in seeing the disciplined sacrificial life which a secular ideology such as Communism could produce on the part of its adherents. Since 1952 there has been a slow growth of the Church so that today it is estimated the membership has risen from approximately 600,000 to 700,000 members. Still an infinitesimal proportion of the total population of the nation, but nevertheless a leaven within the lump.

The second document concerns the relation of church and state. The portion dealing with the posture assumed by Chinese Christians under the Mao regime is a startlingly frank avowal of loyalty both to Christianity and to the Communist government. Let the writer speak for himself:

Christian history in China has not been very long. It is true that Nestorianism came to China in the time of the Emperor T'ai Tsung of the Tang dynasty, 1,300 years ago, and again under the Mongols, 600 years ago, the Christian Church flourished, but it did not take root. The Roman Catholic Church has been here 376 years, from the time when Matthew Ricci began preaching in 1581, the eighth year of Emperor Wan Li, to the present. The Protestant Church has been here only 150 years, from the arrival of Robert Morrison in 1807 until now. As regards numbers, the Catholics now have 3,000,000, and the Protestants less than 1,000,000 members, a very small number in contrast to the 600,000,000 of the population.

Since the Christian Church was brought to China by mission boards and remained under mission-board control, it enjoyed many special privileges as a result of colonialism, but in our national life it never became a political power on its own. The missionary enterprise was made use of by imperialism, and so the history of the church in modern times cannot be separated from the history of imperialism which used the church for purposes of aggression. Reactionary government allied itself to imperialism, and so in the past the Christian Church has consciously or unconsciously served the purposes of reactionary government.

After liberation, imperialism was driven out by the People's Government, the missionaries one after another returned home, and the Chinese Church broke off all relations with imperialism and has gradually become, in fact, self-governing, self-supporting, and self-propagating. After seven or eight years of actual experience, Chinese Christians have come to recognize that the People's Government under the leadership of the Chinese Communist party is sincere in its policy of freedom of religious belief and is helping the church to solve various practical difficulties. . . .

We passionately love our country, we passionately love the People's Government, and we passionately love socialism, because we believe that this kind of state and this kind of government is wholly according to the will of God. As far as we are concerned, there is complete separation of church and state, but without any mutual conflict. The Communists are atheistic, but they respect us who have faith, and the government which they lead will protect religion as long as religion continues to exist. Although we and the Communists differ in faith, we are all Chinese and are one in our desire for the increasing prosperity, strength, and glory of our country. This difference in belief is therefore no hindrance to intimate co-operation in the building up of our country.

Some people in the West on hearing that we love our country are disturbed, fearing that we are becoming narrow nationalists or Chauvinists, and particularly that in loving our country we will cease to love God. This fear is groundless. There are two reasons why we are so patriotic. First, in the past the church was under colonial rule and cut off from the people, who looked upon Christianity as a foreign religion and upon Christians as slaves to a foreign power. Now, from the inception of the Three-Self-Movement in the estimation of the majority of the people the church has become something completely new. Secondly, our country under the leadership of the Communist party is something deserving of love. And so our patriotism is a spontaneous emotion and not a forced manifestation.

Some Western Christians on hearing that we unreservedly support the People's Government have concluded that the Chinese Church has lost its independence. They say that the fact that we cannot oppose the government is a proof that we do not have real freedom. But we recognize that the People's Government is a constitutional government established by the people; its entire policy is based on the interest of the people as a whole and is for the service of the people.

After enumerating the eight points formulated by the Oxford Conference of 1937 as essentials of religious liberty for the Christian Church, the writer declared: "According to our experience the Church in New China has not been interfered with in any of these ways. Western Christians are always raising the point that the church believes in God and Communists do not, and the latter will therefore not allow the Christian Church to continue to exist. But the formal logic of this objection has already been refuted by our experience."

Obviously the Soviet Union and Communist China furnish the most significant evidence of what the actual impact of a Red regime on organized religion may be expected to be. It should be remembered that the dominant Christian communion in the Soviet Union has a historic tendency that is an asset to a totalitarian regime. It appears also in the history of the Lutheran churches. In a word, it effects a harmony between church and state by defining their spheres in a way that minimizes conflict. Church and state are, so to speak, so definitively separate that the result suggests union. There are assumed to be two spheres, the spiritual and the secular, equally under divine rule. The state therefore, in its own sphere, has legitimate authority, even as the church has in its own sphere. The implications of this conceptual distinction for religious life in a Communist regime are obvious. The justification of Christian support of the regime in Communist China, quoted above, is immensely significant as a rationale; it needs to be considered of course in relation to a quite contrary judgment, rendered by one of our most competent and informed observers, that the Chinese Church is now the obedient servant of the government.

Important also is the fact that the theory of the relation of church and state obtaining in the Soviet Union is strictly in accord with the Communist conception of religious liberty. That is to say, the church may not be subversive of the established order which is secularist in the highest degree. The Communists, paradoxically enough, agree with our American conservatives who want the ministers to "stick to the gospel." This is because they fear that if the churches enter the political field they will "rock the boat." This is in accord with the Communist position. Yet something important should be added. Article 124 of the "Great Stalinist Constitution" of 1936 reads: "In order to ensure to citizens freedom of conscience, the church in the U.S.S.R. is separated from the state and the school from the church. Freedom of religious worship and freedom of anti-religious propaganda are recognized for all citizens." The point to be emphasized is that there is no guarantee of freedom of religious propaganda.

121

East Germany

In the course of our study we received and translated into English a manifesto by a group of churchmen in East Germany. This group, representing the Christian Democratic Union (C.D.U.), is small and not representative of the Protestant churches in East Germany, but the statement known as the Meissen declaration is an amazingly significant example of the ease with which orthodox theologians who adhere closely to classical Christian doctrine can convert their theological beliefs into a rationale for wholehearted support of a Communist government. It is, therefore, quoted at some length:

Christian realism is a philosophy according to which, in the light of their faith, Christians look at, evaluate, and adjust to the world. The content of Christian realism is established by the teaching and life of Christ and by the example of the most outstanding and faithful Christians of all ages and all peoples. The theological rationale of the Christian-Democratic Union is Christian realism. . . .

This realistic conception leads irrefutably to the conviction that the Creator, in his infinite goodness, has made available to man, in his senses and intelligence, good and sufficient tools for understanding the world. But it also means that such understanding does not simply happen; striving for knowledge is in itself one of the tasks God has set for man. Part of the belief in God's self-manifestation is recognition of the reliable self-revelation of nature also, into which man constantly deepens his insight through observation and research. The obligation is thus established for man to work constantly for greater understanding of God and his creation. Christians therefore endorse the progress of science and the unremitting exertion implied in such progress.

Because of this realistic approach, Christians come to have a very modest idea of man and his possibilities. It is completely foreign to Christians to regard man as complete in himself or as the measure of all things, despite their appreciation of man as made in God's image. Christians see man, in the light of his sinfulness, as a creature indeed destined for the highest achievement but nevertheless prone to depravity and the most fearful debasement and crime. Christians see man as caught in the tension between the command to make himself master of all the earth and the danger of becoming himself overwhelmed by material things and the power of his own technical achievement. They see man as played upon by both destructive and constructive forces. . . .

All great confessions agree in their belief in Jesus Christ, proclaimed as the Son of God by his resurrection from the dead. When we, as a political party, talk of Christian faith, we do not set ourselves to formulate religious dogma but to apply realistically the substance of Christian belief. The teachings of all Christian confessions are well established, and it is by comparing these that we may isolate those points of doctrine on which all are at one. We believe, with Christians of all confessions, that today it is essential to emphasize what we have in common rather than our differences. . . .

The first word with which Christ began his public career was *Metanoeite*—"change your hearts!" Repentance or change of heart is the precondition for the world's regeneration. Christ represents man as responsible to God. Nor is this responsibility simply an inner, personal matter, but also a public one for God is lord not only of the human heart but of all creation. . . .

Jesus' criticism of his contemporary society is attested to by page after page of the Gospels. With the object of changing existing conditions, Jesus taught the equal rights of all nations as well as the human dignity of slaves, women, and children. Jesus was a help to the poor and oppressed, a savior to the blind and lame, to the deaf, the lepers, and the sick whom nobody else would help in those days. The story of modern social welfare begins with the example of Christ. Jesus warned of the dangers of wealth and set himself with determination against the exploitation of the helpless by the ruling class. . . .

The primitive Christian church of the first three centuries, made up for the most part of proletarian members, evolved in its communities the model of a new way of life based on voluntary love of one's neighbors rather than on coercion and self-seeking. It developed a new standard of social behavior by proclaiming the equality of all nations and classes, as well as by insisting on the use of property as a means of equalizing social opportunities. Thus the church of the martyrs created in its communal living the image of a new order vastly superior to the society existing around it. The Christians of these first three centuries represent for their time the most significant advance guard of social progress. . . .

The Christian social reformers, along with Karl Marx and his followers, were about the only individuals in the nineteenth century who addressed themselves to social problems in all true seriousness, real willingness to help, and readiness to change intolerable conditions. . . .

From the very beginning, Marx correctly evaluated industrialization which had become dominant in Germany, and recognized that the harm done by capitalism could only be decisively repaired by destroying this form of social organization. Without accepting dialectical materialism in its totality, Christians should see that the fundamental economic analysis of Marxism-Leninism is correct. . . .

In its awareness of Christian responsibility, the C.D.U. dedicates itself to the socialistic regeneration of society. Our striving for a new and better social order can profit from the example of Karl Marx and his movement, which has now come to fruition in the Soviet Union. We must therefore continue co-operating with Marxism-Leninism in political solidarity, for the best interests of our people. . . .

The C.D.U., like other democratic forces in Germany, therefore follows the path of co-operation with the great peace camp, now led by the Soviet Union. . . .

Preparations for a third world war, initiated by the U.S.A., force us to come to a clear decision. He who is against imperialist wars must align himself with the peace front of the world.

These lengthy quotations from documents have only one purpose, namely, to make intelligible certain views, states of mind, and patterns of action that are exceedingly difficult for most Christians—and most patriotic Americans—to understand. The third one—the document promulgated by the East German Protestant group—is doubtless far from typical. Presumably, it would be repudiated by the majority in the Russian zone if faced by the necessity of making a choice and if free to make such a judgment. But it is the most striking evidence I have seen of the ease with which a group of churchmen thoroughly grounded in classical Protestantism can erect upon its premises a rationale for loyal support of a Communist regime. The long-standing controversy, involving Karl Barth, over this issue has confronted Protestant church leaders throughout the world with this anomaly. Indeed some would say that the eminent theologian had incurred a large share of the responsibility for the ambivalence of Protestant Christianity overseas with respect to the Communist issue. In his now famous letter to an inquiring East German pastor, Barth wrote:

You speak several times in your letter of your government's obviously increasing "hostility to Christ." This might be so, although this remains an open question. In any event such a "hostility" exists not only in the Communist East but also in the so-called "free" West, though in a different guise. You clearly know that. But you must reckon with this truth and keep it before your eyes day in and day out.[15]

To the question whether Christians can take "the required loyalty oath to the East German Government" Barth replied, in part:

"Loyalty" does *not* mean approval of the ideology on which this government is built. It does not mean approval of each and every measure of the actual officials and representatives of this government. "Loyalty" reserves the right of freedom of thought over against the ideology, and the right of opposition, even of resistance to particular implications and applications of the given system. There is such a thing as a loyal opposition. . . . I would not see any difficulty, were I in your shoes, in offering this loyalty to the East German Republic, and thus in truthfully pledging the oath that is required from you.[16]

Lessons in Cultural Change

Two lessons may be drawn from the many examples that we have found of personal and official accommodation to the Communist rule. One is perhaps sufficiently plain after the evidence reviewed—at tiresome length, the reader may feel—of the exceedingly persuasive appeal, in ethical as well as material terms, Communism has made to peoples who have suffered individual hardship and want and collective indignities, which they are now promised need afflict them no longer if they will make a rational choice. The other lesson is less immediately obvious and harder to learn. It is that Christians who are trying to serve God in a Marxist land and who find the accommodation formula persuasive are acting in a pattern to which we in the West are no strangers. When a minister or an educator faces a moral dilemma which presents him with a "forced option" between compromise

[15] Karl Barth and Johannes Hamel, in *How to Serve God in a Marxist Land* (New York: Association Press, 1959), p. 52. Used by permission.
[16] *Ibid.,* p. 68.

and resignation of his post he does what one or the other group of Christians in Red China, earlier referred to, has done. He makes a complete renunciation, or he compromises and finds a rationale for doing so, and *the latter course may be right.* As our theologians continually remind us, the moral life is filled with ambiguities, and compromise—especially in the political sphere— is often the only alternative to moral defeat. We are today greatly in need of a new perspective on the encounter between Christianity and Communism as devoted men and women are daily experiencing it. An eminent American journalist contributed a letter to our inquiry in which he said:

The acceptance of Christianity has not resulted in a corresponding acceptance of the ideas of Jesus Christ. Christianity represents more an effort to satisfy the spiritual urge than a total commitment to the Christian idea. For example: suppose someone of the planning desk of the State Department were to get up at an important department meeting considering problems of national security and say: "Gentlemen, what would Jesus say?" My guess is that such a man might be led politely by the hand out of the meeting.

There is a sting in that, but a salutary one. Walter Lippmann wrote something very like it about our way of life long before international Communism had reared its head.

6
SOME ISSUES
NEEDING ANALYSIS

It seems in order now to inquire into certain specific issues that continually arise when an attempt is made to evaluate national policy with respect to Communism. Some of these questions are confused and need clarification. Some are rooted in strongly contrasting purposes. They all lend themselves to sloganizing, which impedes clear thinking and evaluation. Let us look at them one by one.

Peaceful Coexistence

The recurrence of the phrase "peaceful coexistence" in policy discussions has a unique aspect in that for the most part the term goes undefined and has no agreed meaning. Such a term must be set over against one or more alternatives if it is to be helpfully discussed. Much of what has been written and spoken on peaceful coexistence as between East and West, between Communism and democracy, between the U.S.A. and the U.S.S.R., seems to imply that the issue is how strong our convictions and commitments are, rather than how workable one or another policy will prove to be. It is as if the challenge "Who is on the Lord's side?" were thrown out with the implication that for all who are there can be no alternative to fighting it out.

Thus peaceful coexistence takes on the color of something cowardly and evil—denoting appeasement, softness toward Communism, and much more that is reprehensible. We read about the "'illusion of peaceful coexistence'" as if the very concept were sheer Communist propaganda. Before me as I write is an example of this kind of argument: "The West is to be sold peaceful coexistence, a Communist concept which means heartfelt, all-out co-operation on your side, tactically measured, carefully controlled reciprocity on mine." [1] Underlying this position, apparently, is an assumption that the cold war must go on regardless of the possibility that it will suddenly become hot and that the alternative to peaceful coexistence will turn out to be peaceful non-existence on both sides of the curtain.

This is surely an unfortunate oversimplification of the whole matter. Perhaps it is a holdover of the "one-world-or-none" idea which, however valid as a distant goal, has no necessary relevance to the world as it is today. As Walter Lippmann has said, "There has never been *one* world."

This is not to contend that there is only one side to the argument over coexistence, even when the concept is thus oversimplified. The debate between Bertrand Russell and Sidney Hook, which attracted much attention, brought two positions into bold relief. Hook took a firm stand for an unrelenting crusade against Communism regardless of the risk of nuclear war. He thought that mutual destruction would be preferable to domination by Communist power. He also thought that only such a posture would be respected by the Kremlin. There is honorable precedent for this position in the memorable declaration of Patrick Henry. Lord Russell, on the other hand, was ready to entrust the matter to history, believing that, at the worst, hope for the human race, or some sizable portion of it, was not so slight as to warrant putting it in such grievous jeopardy. There are Christians among us who formerly rejected all pacifism but are now inclined to take the position Lord Russell took—call it "nuclear pacifism"?—while others choose the "liberty-or-death" alternative.

My own purpose at this point is to make a plea, not for a particular decision but for clarity and consistency in thinking about the East-West encounter. To be sure, the Communist powers are responsible, in the first instance, for the confusion concerning peaceful coexistence that so widely obtains, for they have assimilated it to their propaganda line. This is all the more reason for sober thinking on the subject, however, since it is the

[1] Charles W. Lowry, "U-2—Me Too," *The Blessings of Liberty* (July 1960).

strategy behind the propaganda that must concern us most. Because the Kremlin seems to have a favorite technique of alternately scaring and soothing the non-Communist peoples, a single bit of propaganda may be quite misleading. On balance, it seems probable that the Soviet intention expressed in the coexistence formula is to be understood as follows:

The Soviet Union contemplates war with dread, as we in America do, but is far from ready to forego its major objectives even in the interest of world peace. In the Communist vocabulary a peace-loving nation means of course one that is ready to accommodate itself to the policies of the Communist bloc. Fantastic as it is to our eyes, that is presumably a psychological equivalent of the mood in which we once went to war to "make the world safe for democracy." It is reasonable to assume that those in the Communist bloc who take their ideology seriously equate Communism with democracy by putting all the stress on government *for* the people—as Communist doctrine defines their needs. There is a new factor in the situation, however, in that the hazards of nuclear war dwarf those of the old conventional warfare. Presumably the Soviet Union is as eager to survive as is the United States. Presumably, also, it is as eager to establish Communism throughout the world as our government is to make the Western ideal of freedom prevail. But the Communists have a resource, other than military might, that is not available to us. Both sides depend heavily on armed might—the Communist bloc in order to support its ideological offensive and we in the West in order to defeat it. Communism has a built-in weapon all its own, however—an ideological dogma of inevitable triumph over capitalism in the economic sphere. This apparently unshakable confidence makes it possible to offer peaceful coexistence to the non-Communist world—and *mean* it—in the literal sense of avoiding armed conflict. Given the deterrent of nuclear armament—not absolute, but vastly potent—the Communist states can without dismay, and even with relief, see what they regard as an inevitable struggle shifted from the military to the economic sphere. Indeed, if their experts appraise realistically the balance of military potential, the Communist powers cannot afford to take any other course.

This is of course conjecture, not certainty, but in a precarious age like the present men and nations must often live by conjecture. This is largely what contemporary diplomacy consists of. The line of reasoning above indicated finds a considerable measure of support in the outgivings of Khrushchev. It may be well to look at some of them in this connection.

His most serious attempt at elucidating—and *selling* to Americans—the Soviet idea of peaceful coexistence—a statement that has relatively few Khrushchevian crudities—appeared as the lead article, "On Peaceful Coexistence," in *Foreign Affairs*. It calls for rather extended quotation. The most noteworthy feature of the article is the characterization of peaceful coexistence as competitive. That is to say, it is interpreted as an instrument of Communist policy, national and international, aimed at the same ultimate goal as Soviet military strategy, namely, the triumph of Communism. Khrushchev said:

We Communists believe that the idea of Communism will ultimately be victorious throughout the world, just as it has been victorious in our country, in China and in many other states. Many readers of *Foreign Affairs* will probably disagree with us. Perhaps they think that the idea of capitalism will ultimately triumph. It is their right to think so. We may argue, we may disagree with one another. *The main thing is to keep to the positions of ideological struggle, without resorting to arms in order to prove that one is right.* The point is that with military techniques what they are today, there are no inaccessible places in the world. Should a world war break out, no country will be able to shut itself off from a crushing blow.

We believe that ultimately that system will be victorious on the globe which will offer the nations greater opportunities for improving their material and spiritual life. It is precisely socialism that creates unprecedentedly great prospects for the inexhaustible creative enthusiasm of the masses, for a genuine flourishing of science and culture, for the realization of man's dream of a happy life, a life without destitute and unemployed people, of a happy childhood and tranquil old age, of the realization of the most audacious and ambitious human projects, of man's right to create in a truly free manner in the interests of the people.[2]

[2] October, 1959, 38, No. 1, p. 5. Used by permission.

This passage has been chosen for use here instead of Khru-shchev's explicit definition of peaceful coexistence in the same article for the reason that the latter includes repudiation of war, noninterference in the internal affairs of other countries, and the like—the very sort of Soviet propaganda statements in which the West has lost confidence. In contrast, the economic proposal has the ring of reality, in the light of the existing power situation.

Senator Hubert Humphrey, who had a lengthy interview with the Premier, writes: "Khrushchev has laid his cards on the table. He has given us his blueprint for conquest and has, in effect, said, 'if there's a hydrogen-bomb war, we'll all come out the loser, but we can beat you in the economic, political, and propaganda fields. Let's compete there.' " [3] To be sure, the political and propaganda fields are broad enough to "cover a multitude of sins." The important point is the exclusion of all-out war.

A rather amusing variation on this theme was contained in a speech the Soviet Premier made during his Austrian tour. As reported in an official Soviet journal Khrushchev said:

All of mankind lives on this old planet of ours. To a certain extent the way we live and coexist can be compared to the biblical legends about Noah's Ark. Noah built an ark and took into it seven pairs of clean and two pairs of unclean beasts. Though they did not respect each other they kept their peace in Noah's Ark because they understood that if they did not behave themselves the ark would break up and they would all drown. . . . If on this earth we are not able to get along as the living things put on Noah's Ark, and if we start a war to settle disputes between states—between those that don't like socialism and those that don't like capitalism—we shall destroy our Noah's Ark, the earth. [4]

This unsophisticated, impromptu-sounding, promise-free comment strongly suggests a conscious accommodation to the cold facts of the cold war.

It should go without saying that competitive coexistence of the sort here described is not a formula for *ending* the cold war. At best, it would involve continuation of the struggle between mu-

[3] *Saturday Review* (June 11, 1960), p. 18.
[4] "Visit of Peace and Friendship," *USSR* (November, 1960), p. 2. Used by permission.

tually hostile ideologies, but with nonlethal weapons. It would present a set of strategic problems to which we shall give attention later. The foregoing discussion has been an attempt to clarify the concept as something substantively distinguishable from the political propaganda and diplomatic intrigue at which the Communists are notoriously adept.

"National Interest" and "National Sovereignty"

It is a commonplace that national policy is shaped in accord with some consensus as to what the national interest is. There is no more stubborn reality than the fact of national interest; yet few concepts are harder to define in concrete terms and in balanced fashion. Moreover, the difficulty tends to increase. When Winston Churchill, visiting in America some years ago, was asked to define Great Britain's European policy he was reported as replying, "That is easy: Britain supports the second power on the Continent." It is doubtful if a British statesman would regard that balance-of-power formula as having any considerable relevance to the national interest of Britain today. In William McKinley's day our own country had little difficulty in deciding what the national interest of the United States dictated at any critical point in foreign relations; yet today the question is one of continuous and agonizing concern.

Broadly speaking, this increasing perplexity is an aspect of the steadily growing involvement of nations in each other's affairs—of a new interdependence that continually narrows the range of possible unilateral action. It is a great paradox of history that at a time when nationalism has become an explosive force of unprecedented magnitude international sanctions are in more vocal demand than ever before. Infant nations seek recognition, respect, and a place in the sun under the aegis of the United Nations—limited as the organization is by the great-power veto. The Western powers are actually finding that their prestige and prosperity may be enhanced by drawing back from the pursuit of what they formerly regarded as unquestionable objectives.

This concept of national interest has been the focus of much theological discussion. Like the clash of interest between economic groups, it has been played down by idealists who thought in "harmonistic" terms and who envisioned the end of the "war system" through one great act of collective renunciation. "Realistic" thinkers have warned against the utopian idea that national interests could be so readily harmonized. Reinhold Niebuhr in *Moral Man and Immoral Society*, a book that has profoundly influenced ethical thought for nearly a generation, showed the great difference between the levels of action attained by individuals at their best and what can be looked for in organized group behavior which reflects a common denominator of motive and purpose. This fact no doubt accounts in large part for the low esteem in which politics is commonly held. The political necessity of winning support not only from people who share the outlook of an aspirant to public office, but also from persons who have little regard for broad ethical considerations is a practical dilemma which poses problems that are often disheartening to one who seeks to bring high sanctions to bear on political decisions. Foreign policy is in our day the area of greatest difficulty in this respect.

A consideration of the implications of national sovereignty in this context should be helpful. The nation-wide debate over the proposed Bricker Amendment arose out of a great fear that the government of the United States would suffer a limitation of its freedom of action through treaties and executive agreements negotiated without the sanction of Congress. Merely to put that fear into words is to recognize that treaties and executive agreements do limit a government's freedom of independent action; otherwise there would be nothing to argue about. One might even say that diplomacy is a process by which limitations upon independent action are accepted by governments wanting to get on with each other to their mutual advantage.

Obviously every government that became a member of the United Nations was consciously limiting the range of its unilateral action. Unwillingness to do that on any considerable scale kept the United States out of the League of Nations. Our entrance into the United Nations was evidence that this nation had gained sufficient maturity to see that the unlimited right to act unilaterally is ultimately the right to perish unilaterally.

That is what our extreme nationalists today seem ready to take a chance on. Rather than bear the inconvenience of "hanging together" they accept the risk of "hanging separately."

What has this to do with sovereignty? To act in sovereign fashion is to make deliberate, effective choices between real alternatives. In personal relations we recognize that our substantial freedom is enhanced by devising and accepting rules of behavior that involve renouncing individual liberty—the right to unilateral action—in specified situations. The ordinary rules of courtesy and the many mutual accommodations of neighborly living have this character. In return for the concessions we make we gain a new measure of assurance that our purposes will not be obstructed in matters of greater moment. Have we thereby limited our sovereign character as persons?

Participation in international agreements which recognize the necessity of some measure of joint or collective authority may properly be regarded as the most mature exercise of sovereignty. It is a marked characteristic of adolescence, in nations as in persons, that they identify freedom with the right to act without restraint, to start from scratch in making decisions, unbound by precedent or by any imposed sanction. This is not freedom, however; it is rather a definition of irresponsibility! It is a major quality of Christian ethics that it transmutes individual irresponsibility, often glorified as liberty, into the higher freedom of life in a spiritual community. In secular politics and diplomacy such a community cannot be realized, but it is surely a function of Christian citizenship to make this spiritual principle as fully relevant as possible to the secular order.

In sum, the national interest is the basic guide to policy in the relationships obtaining between nation states, but the content of the concept of national interest alters as changes occur in the factors that condition international relations. Of major importance are the global and regional power structures of the world, but power—even in its crudest aspect as sheer might—is never wholly an end in itself. It is a means to the ends that those who make national policies believe to be worth striving toward. Naked power corrupts itself in the eyes not only of those against whom it is used but also of the peoples on whose behalf governments exercise it. National interest is continually redefining itself in accord with that imponderable force which our fathers called "a decent regard for the opinions of mankind." A gauge of this process of change is the diminishing ratio of the unilateral decisions governments make to the multilateral decisions in which they participate.

Political maturity is manifest not in disregarding or rising above national interest, not in surrendering sovereignty, but in the realization that the long run interest of a nation and the effectual exercise of sovereignty are furthered only as more and more of the peoples of the world who are affected by a given policy are truly and consciously beneficiaries of its execution. If any solution is to be found for the East-West conflict it surely will point in this direction.

Colonialism

Reference was made earlier to the great importance now attaching to colonialism as an issue in the Cold War. The significance of this factor is not so much intrinsic, socially and economically, as it is political. It reflects a restlessness on the part of peoples yearning for nationhood and a lingering resentment on the part of those who have achieved independence but are still smarting from the indignities and injustices which so often characterize colonial regimes. The colonial problem furnishes the Communist world with a ready-made issue for exploitation in the cold war. The issue shaped up in the 1960 UN Assembly, not as a substantive matter, but as one of timing. The action taken on the Soviet proposal for an immediate and unconditional termination of colonialism was highly significant. On the surface a rejection of the Communist demand, it nevertheless revealed the narrowness of the margin of effective support the Western powers could count on in their effort to keep the attainment of national independence a political process rather than make it a matter of political fiat.

It is perhaps not strange, in such a situation, that proposals of vast moment should be framed and acted on by the most important political institution in the world without any serious attempt to define terms or to envisage, operationally, the implementation of a policy adopted. It may be—and this seems probable—that the spokesman for the West relied on the process of implementation to clarify the meaning of the action taken under emotional pressure and to compel all parties to effect a workable agreement. There are situations in which it appears desirable and even necessary to make generalized commitments in terms of policy which must later be spelled out in operational terms, and in an inevitably precarious fashion. The Declaration of Human Rights is an example of this at the international level, as is the U. S. Supreme Court's historic decision in the school-segregation cases at the national level. When such an occasion arises it is of the utmost importance that all relevant questions be patiently scrutinized.

What, then, is meant by "colonialism"? Plainly, it is, in the present controversy, a polemically useful term rather than a definition of policy. If we lift the word out of its present confused context a working definition may be attempted. It should be observed first that the word is not definitive—that is, there is no specific policy corresponding to the term. By the same token, to be a colonial power—to have one or more colonial possessions —is not equivalent to having a specific colonial policy. Moreover, a given power may pursue, at different times and under different conditions, policies that are in sharp contrast.

Secondly, colonies come into a nation's possession in different ways. Conquest is one way, and colonial possessions may be treated as no better than pawns. In contrast, however, title to colonial territory may pass from one nation to another as a result of conflict that affected the colony in no other way than to improve its status. It is doubtful if any competent historian would deny that the status of Cuba after the Spanish-American war was much more desirable than before. In the long run, the Philippines experienced emancipation at the hands of the United States, in spite of grievances legitimately complained of.

There is also, since the creation of the United Nations, the category of trusteeship territories, responsibility for which is multilaterally determined, but administration of which may in some degree approximate the unilateral administration of national colonies.

Thirdly, it has been amply demonstrated that colonial powers differ profoundly in their over-all colonial policies. The most significant criterion is the goal: Indefinite continuance of colonial status or ultimate independence and successful self-government.

Fourthly, and all-importantly from the viewpoint of the Western world, the evils associated with colonialism are more than matched by the imposition of control over a weaker, nominally independent nation by a stronger one and the use of that power in exploitive fashion. This is the crux of the case the United States and Great Britain seek to make against the great Communist powers at the bar of the United Nations.

A meaningful definition of colonialism, therefore, as an evil institution is no longer a definition of legal status, but one of functional political relationships. From an ethical and a politically realistic viewpoint, a satellite may have a status vastly inferior to that of a colonial territory. Recognition of this fact, however, must not obscure the baneful tendency of national power to make administration akin to exploitation and to interpret "readiness for self-government" in prejudicial and unjust fashion.

The Monroe Doctrine

Since the Castro revolution in Cuba a good deal has been heard about the Monroe Doctrine. The matter is relevant here to the extent that there is a threat from abroad to intervene in the affairs of any nation in North or South America. To be sure, that historic doctrine was aimed only at Europe. When in 1823 President Monroe was convinced that European nations, including imperial Russia, had designs on Latin American countries he warned that "we should consider any attempt on their part to extend their system to any portion of this hemisphere, as dangerous to our peace and safety." In this book I have followed the common practice of designating the Communist world as "the East." The Cuban affair is one of many illustrations of the imprecision of that designation, to which reference was made earlier. The Monroe Doctrine, however, is a declaration of policy the significance of which is "in the substance, not the form." Manifestly, the fact that most of the nations to whom Monroe's warning was addressed are now linked to us in some degree as allies in no way limits the implications of the doctrine.

The real issue concerning it arises at another point. The propriety of invoking the Monroe Doctrine as a prelude to implementing it depends on answers to questions like these: In view of the intervening history is such a hemispheric protectorate practicable and acceptable to the other American states involved? In view of the Charter of the Organization of American States, the Treaty of Rio de Janeiro (1947), and the Caracas Declaration (1954), all of which signalized what has been called the coming of age of the Latin American republics, how much latitude does the United States have in dealing with matters affecting their independence? More serious still, how is the question of possible recourse to the Monroe Doctrine affected by the possible consequences, undreamed of in 1823, of an attempt to enforce it?

These questions are not rhetorical, for just as doctrines defining foreign policy originate in concrete situations in order to ward off specific threats, so they are subject to review, revision, or abandonment when the international scene is significantly altered. In great national emergencies precedents are often shattered and agreements dissolved away without troubling the consciences of statesmen. The point here is that ethics as applied to national policy makes one supreme demand upon governments: Regardless of formal obligations and conventional precedents—which history shows to be viable only when in line with basic political and economic realities—critical decisions must be made in the light of the fullest possible appraisal of the probable consequences for all the peoples concerned of the course of action proposed. It is startling evidence of the gravity of the world situation that men and women of equal probity and intelligence are found on opposite sides of momentous issues, although one or the other side is very likely to be egregiously, perhaps catastrophically, wrong.

Nevertheless, it hardly seems debatable that such a resolution as was introduced in the 86th Congress to put more bite in the

Monroe Doctrine involves extreme hazard. The proposed declaration by the Congress that the United States would be "justified . . . in taking steps to forestall intervention, domination, control and colonization by international Communism in the New World" has, prima facie, possibilities of international mischief-making of which, happily, the State Department seemed to be aware. Moreover, is not a generalization warranted, in this era of rapid and unpredictable change, to the effect that the making of crucial decisions on the part of governments by invoking precedents or historic "doctrines" has built-in hazards against which statesmen should be always on guard? Constructive statesmanship stresses continuity of policy with respect to the maintenance of the national ethos, reinterpretation of previous policy declarations when the times call for it, and abandonment of policies that can no longer express authentically the national interest. Frozen policy is never a national asset.

The U. S. State Department has stressed the role of the Organization of American States as supporting the principle of the Monroe Doctrine in the context of contemporary events: "The principles which the U. S. Government enacted in the face of the attempts of the old imperialism to intervene in the affairs of the hemisphere are as valid today for the attempts of the new imperialism." The question arises, however, whether the warning given to the Soviet Union that a U.S.-Cuban treaty is none of its business is either appropriate or shrewd in view of the fact that our government is making Soviet dealings with small states very much its own affair—and rightly so. The Russian government habitually tries to have it both ways. Should not the Western powers avoid all appearance of encouraging it?

There is a subtle danger here, for the kind of hostile activity we complain of is of a sort difficult to define and proscribe. Overt acts of aggression may be avoided by a nation waging a cold war, consequently any kind of retaliation may look to other governments as all of a piece with the provocation complained of. This is the trouble with the newly invented concept of "indirect aggression," which Walter Lippmann has well said is but another name for cold war. Such hostility may take the form of trade restrictions, immigration bans, even the avowal of a purpose to abet the overthrow of a foreign political regime—by methods short of war. Our own government has at times pursued such policies. Indirect aggression can be forcibly resisted only by turning cold war into hot war. Conceivably, enforcement—especially if unilateral—of the Monroe Doctrine might precipitate armed conflict of unpredictable scope and intensity.

Diplomatic Recognition

Again we find ourselves inevitably involved, by the nature of the subject under exploration in this book, in a highly controversial issue; namely, the question of policy with reference to diplomatic recognition of a revolutionary government—specifically Communist China. Practically speaking, proposed recognition of Red China by the United States government and proposed admission of it to the United Nations—whether as *the* Chinese nation or in addition to Nationalist China—are virtually two phases of one issue as far as the U. S. is concerned; that is to say, opposite judgments on these points, while doubtless possible, would be difficult to reconcile as aspects of an integrated foreign policy.

The purpose and scope of this volume exclude any attempt to judge the issues here raised. On the other hand it seems important that consideration be given to what this country's policy with respect to recognition has been, historically, and what it is today. If the ensuing discussion is disproportionately detailed, its length seems to be justified by the obvious gravity of the matter.

It can hardly be disputed that a major national weakness in the United States is lack of knowledge—and of concern—with respect to the origin and relative consistency of the various aspects of foreign policy, of which diplomatic recognition is one of the most important. I approach the problem here without any prejudgment as to the matters in controversy except for a strong impression that United States policy with respect to diplomatic recognition is very much in need of a clear and explicit statement, and especially of a plain account of the changes it has undergone. It is one of the grievous aspects of what may be called the democratic situation that the people are called upon to choose between proposed alternatives which may have momentous consequences without any clear understanding of what has been happening in the realm of policy making or even of what the official posture of the government is on a particular question at a particular time.

Our State Department in January, 1954, and again in August, 1958, issued statements on the question of recognizing Communist China—the former an officially authorized pamphlet, the latter a formal policy statement. The pamphlet has a section explaining the nonrecognition policy, in which the following paragraph appears:

To start with, let us take a look at the four generally accepted criteria which a new regime ordinarily must meet before its recognition as a legitimate government and its acceptance into the sisterhood of nations. These four criteria are (1) effective control over the territory of the country; (2) sovereign independence; (3) truly representative character—something in the nature of a mandate from the people governed, or at least their consent without coercion; and (4) acceptance of its inherited and generally recognized treaty and other international obligations and adherence to a pretty well established minimum standard of decency in its treatment of foreign nationals and interests within its borders.

These are predominantly *de facto* criteria and in line with what has been held to be the historic American theory of diplomatic recognition, as I shall attempt to indicate below. The writer of the pamphlet holds that in the particular case under examination, that of Communist China, only the first criterion is met. Thus it is possible to justify nonrecognition by reference to traditional concepts, assuming a valid construction of the factual situation.

On the following page of the pamphlet we read:

On grounds of international law, the case against recognition is very strong. On practical grounds, the argument is equally strong.

Recognition has assumed a political and psychological significance which is new. It has become a symbol. Recognition in this case would

141

mean in the eyes of millions, especially in Asia, not necessarily approval but acceptance, accommodation, and reconcilement.

This passage would seem to suggest a change of position which becomes quite explicit in the policy statement of August 11, 1958. In that document we read: "In the view of the United States diplomatic recognition is a privilege and not a right. Moreover, the United States considers that diplomatic recognition is *an instrument of national policy* which it is both its right and its duty to use in the enlightened self-interest of the nation." (Italics added.)

Having thus set forth the primary consideration, the policy statement proceeds at once to apply the traditional criteria, introducing them as secondary considerations: "However, there is reason to doubt that even by the tests often cited in international law the Chinese Communist regime qualifies for diplomatic recognition." It is stated that U. S. policy with respect to recognition of Communist China is "based on a carefully considered judgment of the national interest." Where that judgment leads is quite as explicitly set forth: "The United States holds the view that Communism's rule in China is not permanent and that it one day will pass. *By withholding diplomatic recognition from Peiping it seeks to hasten that passing.*" (Italics added.)

It would be misleading to represent these documents as lacking an appeal to ethical sanctions. The fact that their conclusions are arrived at in relation to what is commonly called international Communism makes it natural to identify nonrecognition with condemnation of ruthless and unscrupulous policies and practices. The question inevitably arises, however, how the current definition of U. S. policy with respect to diplomatic recognition as primarily a matter of national interest can be reconciled with a historic American tradition of *de facto* recognition to which our government has long regarded itself as adhering in principle since it was defined by Thomas Jefferson.

The record of the United States is, of course, not wholly consistent in this respect, but authorities cited by the State Department strongly intimate that its policy statement of August 11,

1958, is essentially a departure from a rather carefully nurtured national tradition.

Charles Cheney Hyde in his monumental work on international law maintained that the *de facto* criterion announced by Jefferson for determining the entitlement of a government to recognition—"the will of the nation, substantially declared"—was observed, in general, down to the time of Woodrow Wilson.[5] In the words of James Buchanan, when Secretary of State: "In its intercourse with foreign nations the Government of the United States has, from its origin, always recognized *de facto* governments. . . . We do not go behind the existing Government to involve ourselves in the question of legitimacy. It is sufficient for us to know that a government exists capable of maintaining itself; and then its recognition on our part inevitably follows." [6]

President Pierce made a similar declaration, adding that when "the people and the public authorities" of the country in question have acted, "their determination, whether it be by positive action or by ascertained acquiescence, is to us sufficient warrant of the legitimacy of the new government." [7] In this connection Hyde himself observes: "Popular approval of a particular régime appears, however, to have been regarded as reasonable deduction from the fact of success rather than as a condition of which the existence remained to be established by special tests of American devising." [8]

G. H. Hackworth, another eminent authority on international law, has summarized the matter thus:

With the possible exception . . . [of certain instances mentioned, involving special circumstances] the policy of recognition prior to the beginning of the administration of President Wilson uniformly followed the fundamental principles laid down by Jefferson . . . [It was implicit in Jefferson's statement that] a government, such as he described, would be in possession of the machinery of government, would possess stability, and would be able and willing to meet its international obligations.

[5] *International Law: Chiefly as Interpreted and Applied by the United States* (2nd rev. ed., Boston: Little, Brown & Company, 1945), I, 161.
[6] *Ibid.,* p. 162.
[7] *Ibid.,* p. 162.
[8] *Ibid.,* p. 162.

Therefore, stipulations to that effect contained in more recent instructions to our diplomatic officers may be regarded as specifically stating conditions which otherwise would have been implied in the principles enunciated by Jefferson.[9]

Instructive also is an official letter by Secretary of State Hull in May, 1936, in which he said:

The special policy pursued by the United States during a part of the period since 1906 with reference to the recognition of governments coming into power in disregard of *constitutional* procedure, has assumed a political importance which has tended to obscure the pattern of uniformity obtaining in the practice of recognition in other instances. Aside from this prerequisite of "constitutionalism" adopted in the recognition of Central American governments and inaugurated by President Woodrow Wilson with reference particularly to certain other of the American republics, the prerequisites during this period have conformed substantially to the so-called *de facto* policy of recognition instituted by Jefferson.[10]

The policy formulated by President Wilson was epitomized by him in a declaration in February, 1917, concerning the existing regime in Costa Rica. The United States, he said, "will not give recognition or support to any Government which may be established unless it is clearly proven that it is elected by legal and constitutional means." [11]

This statement, which was illustrative of Wilson's moralistic viewpoint, appears, in the light of subsequent history, to have been a counsel of perfection. Secretary of State Hughes in a letter to Samuel Gompers in July, 1923, wrote: "We are not concerned with the question of the legitimacy of a government as judged by European standards. We recognize the right of revolution and we do not attempt to determine the internal concerns of other States. . . . [This Government] has never insisted that the will of the people of a foreign State may not be manifested by long con-

[9] Address quoted by Hyde. *Ibid.*, pp. 164-65.
[10] *Ibid.*, p. 166.
[11] *Ibid.*, p. 168.

tinued acquiescence in a régime actually functioning as a government." [12]

There is contained also, however, in Hughes' letter a passage which would presumably be included in a complete documentation of the State Department's present position. He said:

> But while a foreign régime may have securely established itself through the exercise of control and the submission of the people to, or their acquiescence in, its exercise of authority, there still remain other questions to be considered. *Recognition is an invitation to intercourse.* It is accompanied on the part of the new government by the clearly implied or express promise to fulfill the obligations of intercourse. These obligations include, among other things, the protection of the persons and property of the citizens of one country lawfully pursuing their business in the territory of the other and abstention from hostile propaganda by one country in the territory of the other. In the case of the existing régime in Russia, there has . . . been . . . a repudiation of the obligations inherent in international intercourse and a defiance of the principles upon which alone it can be conducted. . . . The sentiment of our people is not deemed to be favorable to the acceptance into political fellowship of this régime so long as it denies the essential basis of intercourse and *cherishes, as an ultimate and definite aim, the destruction of the free institutions which we have laboriously built up, containing as they do the necessary assurances of the freedom of labor upon which our prosperity must depend.*[13]

It appears that Hughes was occupying a position somewhere between Jefferson and Wilson. Even so, Hyde comments on the above statement that the reason for Hughes' "adamant" stand on nonrecognition of the Soviet Union was probably "the organized effort in which he had reason to believe it was engaged to subvert and injure American institutions." [14] Be that as it may, when diplomatic recognition was accorded to the Soviet Union by Franklin D. Roosevelt in 1933 the major concerns expressed by Hughes were included in the stipulations made by our government. Of this event Hyde said: "The recognition in Novem-

[12] *Ibid.,* pp. 170-71.
[13] *Ibid.,* pp. 171-72. Italics added.
[14] *Ibid.,* p. 172.

ber, 1933, of the existing government of Russia stands out as an instance where the United States demanded and secured from a European power unique assurance that it would hold itself in leash as a respecter of international law, and so respond to certain requirements in that regard that previous administrations of the American government had resolutely stood for." [15]

Hyde's over-all conclusion concerning U. S. policy with respect to recognition of foreign governments was that, despite some instances pointing in another direction, "the United States appears at the present time [1945] to be indisposed to employ its recognition policy as a means of intervention in civil strifes within foreign territory. . . . In a word, the policy of the United States in relation to the recognition of new governments appears to be no longer associated with, or made the handmaiden of intervention." [16]

It is not intended in this discussion to suggest that criteria for diplomatic recognition should always remain the same, or should be inflexible. It *is* suggested that U. S. policy in this matter cannot now be accurately defined as *de facto,* or Jeffersonian, in the light of public announcement that nonrecognition of Communist China is an "instrument of national policy." Clarification of the whole matter is overdue.

The important thing is that present policy seems to be at variance with that indicated by the authorities quoted above, whom the public has been allowed to regard as accepted interpreters of the position of our government. We now need a clear and authoritative interpretation of the development of our recognition policy in all its phases.

"Neutralism"

We had better face it; neutralism is a prejudicial word. I have put it in quotes in the caption because it has become current in relation to the cold war in an ill-considered way. An exchange between the New York *Times* and Quincy Wright, an eminent authority on international law, has pointed up the difficulty.

[15] *Ibid.,* p. 177.
[16] *Ibid.,* p. 182.

The *Times* (October 8, 1960), in an editorial on "Neutrality vs. Neutralism," downgraded neutralism as a kind of irresponsibility —in contrast to neutrality.

"It is one thing," said the editorial, "to be 'neutral' in the traditional military sense, avoiding both alliances and involvement in a military conflict. It is quite another thing to be 'neutralist' in the sense of avoiding not only military but also moral involvements and putting expediency above principle." The intimation seemed to be that neutralism, correctly defined, involves imputation to a country of a fault in the national character. The United States, it was pointed out, "pursued a neutral policy" up to the First World War, but, the *Times* contended, "It was never 'neutralist' in its sentiments or actions to the point of aiding the enemy of freedom." The writer of the editorial seemed to overlook the fact that until the United States decided to enter the First World War our posture of neutrality was resented by many Europeans, whose cause we later made our own, for the very reason that the United States seemed to be revealing this unworthy trait of "neutralism."

Wright in a letter commenting on the editorial inverted, so to speak, the *Times*' twofold definition: Neutrality, he said, in the present world scene, "is inconsistent with 'collective security' under the United Nations Charter unless special exceptions are made. . . . India, Sweden and other 'neutralist' countries have recognized this obligation and were not 'neutral' during the hostilities in Korea, Hungary and elsewhere." In this view neutrality is only exceptionally the norm of approved action in the system of international relations established by the UN Charter.

Neutralism, on the other hand, said Wright, "means observance of the principle that everyone should be presumed innocent until proved guilty." The neutralist nations have adopted a position in relation to the East-West conflict resting on the assumption that holding a particular ideology or maintaining a particular political or economic system may not per se be equated to the violation of international obligations. Said Wright: "The 'neutralist' countries have declined to assume in advance that the United States, the Soviet Union, or any other country is intending to embark upon an aggression or other violation of the

147

Charter before an incident arises, and have therefore refused to enter alliances or collective defense arrangements directed against particular states."

Nations may, and do at times, adopt a neutralist attitude toward a dispute through self-interest untempered by a sense of moral obligation. It sometimes happens, however, that a sounder moral judgment of the issue is forthcoming from those who can view the matter from an external vantage point. No long-established nation can consistently, in the light of its own history, condemn another for "neutralism" that is dictated by a bred-in-the-bone conception of national interest.

In the present world situation harsh judgments upon neutralism on the part of governments that are unready to become involved are widely regarded as ill-conceived. Moreover, they seem to be ineffectual and productive of resentment. Where distinction between bloc members and non-bloc members is called for, "uncommitted" would seem to be the more appropriate term.

The Problem of Ends and Means

"The end does not justify the means." It would be hard to name another adage which, while embodying an important ethical principle, is so shot through with ambiguity as is this. Its relevance to our subject is of course obvious. The last word in moral condemnation is the charge that a person, an association, or a government accepts the proposition that "the end justifies the means."

Yet nothing is more evident on reflection than that a "means" is always by definition a "means to an end." "Means," in this context, has no meaning except a method, or instrumentality, of attaining an end. The adage under examination points unquestionably to an important truth, but it puts the matter very confusingly. The solid essence of it is that to disregard the bearing of the means upon the end is to risk the corruption of the end by the means. The ethical obligation to consider continually whether the means—the method, the instrumentality—one proposes to employ can be expected to lead to the contemplated end or is more likely to make the end unattainable.

The major moral defect of the Communist philosophy is the failure to take account of the paralyzing and corrupting effect of concentrated power—in theological terms, the demonic character of all man's devices and institutions which invests them with a strong inclination to subordinate high purposes to unworthy purposes, ultimate ends to proximate ends, thus adulterating good with evil. Perhaps we might say that the significance of the doctrine of original sin is that there is something in human motivation analogous to what economists know as Gresham's law: Debased money drives out sound money. This is not a generalization about human nature in itself so much as about the human situation. To paraphase a well-known scriptural saying, Man is born unto *struggle,* as the sparks fly upward. Existentially, man and his institutions are involved in a competitive struggle for survival and security. It is in this situation that power sincerely organized for human emancipation and betterment may quickly degenerate into the very opposite of what it set out to be. This is why Max Nomad, surveying the long history of the social revolution out of which Communism has come, was constrained to pronounce revolution intrinsically evil. And this, in turn, is why it is a grave ethical error to concentrate on means to the neglect of ends, for only by reference to ends can the means be validated, and surely a great variety of means employed by men and by society must be pronounced cruel and barbarous except as the ends served give them a legitimate character. The crowning example is the total war we have strained every nerve to prosecute with success. Ends and means interpenetrate. To divorce either from the other is perilous, but the tendency to do this is universal.

7
TOWARD A VALID STRATEGY
FOR MEETING
THE COMMUNIST CHALLENGE

Up to this point we have been surveying facts—contemporary and historical—relevant to our study. We have contemplated the phenomenally rapid growth and rapid spread of the Communist movement. We have attempted an interpretation of Communism and its appeal to persons and communities whose background and environment might be expected to make them immune to it. We have considered Communist methods and tactics, and noted the influence of Communism upon religion. We have undertaken to analyze some of the more complex and involved issues which the remarkable growth of this revolutionary movement raises. We need now to inquire, in the light of our faith and value system, what the response of the West and in particular of our own country to the Communist challenge should be and what role the churches should play in this momentous encounter.

We have all learned a great deal from many sources about the Communist line. What should be our line, here in this land that we cherish as a major part of the "Free World"? What resources and procedures for meeting Communism are consistent with our cultural and spiritual heritage, and are likely to be effectual? What possibly tempting strategies should be avoided? What has the Christian ethic—and the ethic of Western democracy—to say to persons and institutions behind the Iron Curtain who are striving to preserve both life and integrity about what should be "rendered unto Caesar"? To what extent and by what means can the Christian witness and Christian evangelism with its personal, man-to-man approach be fruitfully employed in the encounter with Communism? We must come to grips with such questions as these, albeit with serious and teachable humility rather than with dogmatic sureness, with courage but without rashness, with zeal that is tempered by patience, and above all with a personal dedication that will match that which, we have been told again and again, is a conspicuous trait of the disciplined Communist character.

In the preceding paragraph I have put the term "Free World" in quotes. This was symbolic of a deep concern that we in the West shall develop a strategy vis-à-vis Communism that gives no hint of self-righteousness. Our world is not wholly free; the Communist world is not wholly a slave world. It is arguable that we would stand a better chance of breaking through the insensitivity that we so greatly deplore in Communism if we were courageous enough to admit candidly the dark blots on our own record, in race relations, for example, and plead for a joint effort between East and West to set our respective households in order. Suppose we should address our Communist adversaries in the cold war after the fashion of Paul, who exhorted his Christian friends "not as one who has already attained" but as a struggling sinner. There is something more than a little disturbing in the way we assume that our Western civilization is the light of the world!

This study has led me and those collaborating with me to some generalizations that I am constrained to set down before coming to specific elements of a valid strategy. They have to do with "mind set," basic assumptions, and "posture" in this age of crisis.

Facing Realities

First of all, it is necessary to face facts realistically in a time of rapid change. One must be guided by conviction, not paralyzed by moral sentiment and nostalgia. It is doubtful if anyone is equipped to conserve authentic values in a revolutionary age who has not accepted the fact that the future is bound to be different —for most of us perhaps uncomfortably different—from the past, as a result of the social and political ferment that is now working

151

throughout the world. A noted anthropologist has said that cultural change is continuous and inevitable, but also painful. This is a way of calling attention to the persistent conservatism of human society, a prime concern of which is preservation of the structure necessary to give stability to the social order. We in the United States have a way of glorifying revolution in our history while trembling at the thought of any major change in our own time. This attitude no doubt serves as a wholesome cultural gyroscope in view of the importance of continuity in the institutions of mankind. Indeed, it is not implausible to contend that revolution, in the cataclysmic sense of the term, is inherently destructive of human values and, at the most, a second-best way to bring about necessary change.

The Evil in Revolutions

In Max Nomad's book referred to earlier there is a shrewd and rather harsh characterization of political and social revolution. He says:

For between the capitalist hell of wage slavery and the socialist, Communist, syndicalist, or anarchist heaven of social and economic equality, there stands the inevitable transitional phase with its dictatorial or democratic bureaucracy, its military officers and its technical experts, all of whom will insist upon the necessity of a strong government and of higher emoluments and softer jobs for the owners of superior brains. And the transitional phase becomes "transitional" only in a cosmic sense, for its beneficiaries will use their newly acquired power for the purpose of perpetuating that "phase," until a new revolution ushers in a new transitional phase, with another set of "transitional" officeholders.[1]

This brings forcibly to mind Lord Acton's well-known aphorism concerning the corruptive influence of power. One might call it Nomad's Law. It is not political conservatism; quite the contrary. Elsewhere Nomad comments:

Utopian illusions may be a sweet consolation to some, just as religious mysticism is to others. But those of a stronger mold can "bear

[1] *Op. cit.*, p. 160. Used by permission of the author.

all naked truth." Champions of permanent protest, they will keep on fighting for justice, even though its full victory is not within the biological scheme. And the underdog, though he may never see the millennium, will get more out of this life if he keeps on struggling and mistrusting both his masters and his "emancipators." [2]

The former Yugoslav leader Djilas, whose book *The New Class* depicts the corruption of a revolutionary "elite" as a consequence of the concentration of arbitrary power in a relatively small leadership group, seems to arrive at the same negative conclusion with reference to revolution as a method of social regeneration.

Realism in Revolution

All this is important and challenging. It depicts an inescapable hazard of living in a time like ours. Such a contention, however, affords no valid support of the view that since revolution is intrinsically corruptive it is incumbent upon "legitimate" governments or upon the society of nations to crush it wherever it appears. Thomas Jefferson's often-quoted remark, "A little rebellion, now and then, is a good thing," was aimed at this undiscriminating attitude, which takes no account of the fact that when the public welfare is long neglected by a political regime responsible for it the only corrective available may be extralegal force directed against the existing government. At such a time—to cite an event in our own history—"If this be treason, make the most of it" becomes relevant. Moreover—and this is the major consideration—when social revolution for such a purpose is actually under way, its suppression, whether by the domestic government or by foreign intervention, is likely to cause social retardation. One may therefore believe that though revolution is inherently corrupting it is nevertheless inevitable in certain historical situations, where it must be accepted and adjusted to. To the most discriminating observers this appears to be true of the contemporary social revolution in a large part of the world.

The point I am trying to make was illustrated by an officer of our State Department in an address given a few years ago on "China and the Communist Peace Offensive." Referring to the

[2] *Ibid.*, p. 11.

Asian problems created by the Chinese Revolution he said: "I fear I bring no quick, magic formulae for their resolution. There aren't any. In fact, I believe that we are all becoming convinced of—and reconciled to—the unpleasant fact that Asia is going to be throwing problems at us for a long, long time to come."

"Most Asians," he said, become "painfully aware" of unsupplied basic material needs, "and their determination to achieve them as quickly as possible has created in our time forces which even without the disruptive and destructive influence of Communism would be changing the face of that continent where half the people of the world live." [3]

"The Wrath of Men"

The biblical proverb, "They have sown the wind, and they shall reap the whirlwind" is apt in this connection, if in place of the personal pronoun we substitute "a nation," or "society." Not only so, but there is a bit of theology in the Old Testament which has instructive relevance here and which has not been wholly lost on perceptive Christians who found themselves "captives" of one or another of the totalitarian regimes that have darkened Europe and Asia during the present century. When a Christian minister or educator in Red China or in the Russian zone of Germany refers to Communists as in some sense carrying out a divine mission, he may be saying nothing other than Isaiah said when he attributed to the Almighty the words, "Ho, Assyria, rod of mine anger!" To the prophet's mind there was no incongruity in making the wrath of the cruel invader to "praise" God, for he who thus becomes an instrument of divine judgment will, in his turn, fall under judgment for his part in the drama, because in his heart he "meaneth it not so," but is bent only on achieving his private ends.

Whether looked at from a strictly biblical or from a secular viewpoint, all this has in it a logic of history. For those who sing, "This is my Father's world," however, there is a certain impiety in pronouncing any portion of its history wholly evil and in consigning the makers of that history to outer darkness. No po-

---

[3] Alfred le S. Jenkins, Office of Chinese Affairs, December, 1954.

litical or social revolutionary regime to which great masses of human beings have given their allegiance at grievous cost in hardship and suffering is totally evil.

Universal Values

By the same token, it is unjust to condemn the peoples involved as depraved and without any moral sensitivity, responsive only to the argument of force and violence. This is a matter of the utmost importance in the East-West encounter, for what is at stake is the most basic of our Christian—and our democratic—assumptions: The essential oneness of the human race. It is true that there has been a Soviet line castigating all forms of "cosmopolitanism" and that Chinese Communist authority has been cited to the effect that there are no universal values—only values that inhere in class membership. But these are precisely points of contradiction between Christianity and Communism, as the latter is propagated by some of its apostles. It is probably much more accurate to say that Communist messianism contemplates emancipation as inclusive and total. In any case, if we exclude Communists from the community of responsible human beings we shall be violating one of the major propositions of Christianity and one of the major insights of enlightened anthropology.

The late Ralph Linton, an eminent anthropologist, about ten years ago set down some generalizations concerning the great "thematic" values that characterize the various cultures of the world. His schematization presents a sort of continuum of cultures, and is revealing in several respects:

1. All societies share many of the same thematic values although they differ greatly in the patterns by which these are implemented. These values are essentially the same in "primitive" economic systems as in our own.

2. The necessity for satisfying the basic physiological needs of the individual and group, i.e., of providing adequate food, shelter, etc., for a large majority of the society's members, is the starting point for all economic systems.

3. As technology improves, the importance of these physiological

155

needs as determinants of the forms of economic systems diminishes.

4. They are replaced by psychological motivations, desires for prestige or power, desire for aesthetic satisfactions, reinforcement of group solidarity, etc.

5. The most drastic differences between our own and "primitive" economic systems seem to stem less from our technological advance than from the lessening in our society of intimate social contacts and enduring associations.

6. These have led to increasing emphasis on the values which can be most easily associated with individuals, as power and prestige or personal wealth as a symbol of prestige expressing itself in display.

7. Our classical economic concepts of labor as merely another commodity and of the desire for profit as the only motive for economic activity are valid only for societies in which the interactions of individuals, economic and otherwise, have become depersonalized. They do not hold where relations between individuals extend beyond simple economic interactions.[4]

A most emphatic discrediting of the class theory of values is this statement by George P. Murdock, formerly professor of anthropology at Yale University:

The essential unanimity with which the universal culture pattern is accepted by competent authorities, irrespective of theoretical divergences on other issues, suggests that it is not a mere artifact of classificatory ingenuity but rests upon some substantial foundation. This basis cannot be sought in history, or geography, or race, or any other factor limited in time or space, since the universal pattern links all known cultures, simple and complex, ancient and modern. It can only be sought, therefore, in the fundamental biological and psychological nature of man and in the universal conditions of human existence.[5]

The first of Linton's propositions is all-important, laying as it does a basis for an enduring and productive system of relations between human societies. Among the others the seventh is the

---

[4] Unpublished memorandum. I probably should confess that my justification for reproducing this seven-point statement in full is in part the fact that it is relevant not only to the thesis here put forward, but to grievous intergroup conflicts in the United States.

[5] *Ibid.*

most arresting as an indication of the prevalence both of a too rigid and mechanistic economic structure and of the lack of a broader basis for organization of the interests and activities of mankind.

Linton concluded his statement with some words that may well find a similar place in the discussions to which this book is devoted:

> The most valuable contribution of the Church toward the solution of modern economic problems would be in the creation of a really integrated society with common values and a universal sense of responsibility toward each other. Christianity arose in a period when the social disintegration was as great as it is at present, and it managed to accomplish this among its converts. Can it do the same thing again? [6]

"Anti-Communism" Is Not Enough

In many ways the Communist world confronts us as the pagan world, and religious faiths alien to Christianity faced our missionaries in the early stages of the missionary movement. The initial and natural response was characterized by zeal to make converts—which has never abated—accompanied by a strongly negative attitude toward the indigenous religion found in a missionary field. The strategy of the resulting approach was one which William Ernest Hocking has called "radical displacement" and criticized as ill-adapted to the realities of the cultural situation.[7] That is to say, the aim was to substitute a new religion for whatever religion prevailed.

While no one strategy prevails throughout the missionary enterprise today, it is not too much to say that to an impressive degree missionary leaders, including secretaries of the Christian associations stationed abroad, have cultivated a different approach from that just referred to. This approach in no way weakens loyalty to the faith they were commissioned to represent—quite the contrary—but the modified approach was productive of respect for the native culture and a positive attitude toward its

---

[6] *Ibid.*

[7] *Living Religions and a World Faith* (New York: The Macmillan Company, 1940). Hibbert lectures, 1938.

values. Is there not an instructive precedent here for a Christian approach to Communism? If we take from Christianity its historic universality—its imputation of worth and spiritual potentiality to all sorts and conditions of men—it is no longer Christianity. The Communists are part of the human race, however dangerously misguided we believe them to be. Any strategy resting on a contrary assumption is bound to be ineffectual. One of our most perceptive and well-informed younger theologians has written:

A polemical response to the challenge of Communism is in one sense the oldest and most natural reaction for the Christian world. From the time of the younger [pre-materialist] Marx, Christians have met the Marxist attack on religion by . . . condemning Communism as atheistic in theory and immoral in practice, and by defending as one united whole their faith and their "Christian civilization." . . . This kind of anti-Communism fights a blind rearguard action against the rapidly changing realities of today.[8]

And one of the best informed missionary leaders in America wrote:

When the Communist devotee calls our faith unscientific, superstitious, and antisocial, we do not answer him with a denunciation of his atheism. There is too much practical atheism outside of the Communist camp. Rather, we endeavor to make real to the Communist our faith that gives true meaning and value to life, a faith that is not measured by mortal minds alone, but dares to trust in the holy mysteries of infinity and eternity, a faith that rescues man from proud, self-righteous deification of his own achievements. . . . Some day, we pray, his antireligious scorn may change to humble and devout reverence.[9]

It should go without saying that Christianity is hostile to Communism on religious grounds and shares with democracy the

[8] From *Communism and the Theologians*, Charles C. West. © SCM Press Ltd., 1956. By permission of The Westminster Press and SCM Press Ltd.

[9] Reprinted with permission of McGraw-Hill Book Company, Inc. from "Christian Presuppositions for the Encounter with Communism" by Frank W. Price in *The Theology of the Christian Mission*, ed. by Gerald H. Anderson. Copyright © 1961 by Gerald H. Anderson.

latter's hostility to that movement on social and philosophical grounds. A movement which has the idealistic and political appeal that we have found to characterize Communism as a large part of the world's population sees it cannot be successfully countered by a simple and absolute negation, however. Moreover, an all-out fight of this sort against a movement—or a person—presupposes what has been called the "devil theory of history," which is quite unsound both philosophically and theologically. On the whole, this approach is not only self-defeating in dealing with nations and mass movements; it reflects something much less than a Christian perspective.

There is a broad Christian consensus to the effect that in some circumstances a nation is justified in taking up arms against another. Waging war, hot or cold, however, against a world-wide movement is like trying to restrain an ocean tide. It is one of the most melancholy features of our American policy in the present struggle that we departed from the principle—once laid down by John Foster Dulles himself, before he became Secretary of State—that American policy in relation to the U.S.S.R. should not be directed against a system of social and economic organization as such, but rather against any imperialist drive to impose that system on other nations. Yet we have noted in the preceding chapter the official abandonment of this well-taken position. Our national policy in relation to Communism is frankly declared to be aimed at the destruction of the numerically greatest political regime in the world—Communist China. We do not need to be moralistic about this: A cold war, like a hot war, entails in some degree a moratorium on traditional moral sanctions. The immediate point is that in great part the prevailing posture of the West toward Communism is ineffectual.

No question is raised here as to the intrinsic hostility of Communism to religion. Putting aside all argument concerning the essence of religion, or the validity of the concept of a secular religion, we must face frankly the fact that though Communist practice may vary in accord with the particular situation faced, the official Communist doctrine is antitheistic and hostile to all traditional religion of whatever form. We saw earlier, however, that very commonly this atheism seems to play no part, or a negligible part, in a country with a strong Catholic tradition—Italy, for example—in the decision whether or not to vote the Communist ticket. Broadly speaking, the Communist issue, in countries where the movement is above ground, tends to resolve itself into a practical, political choice, to which religion is considered irrelevant. On the other hand, we all know many devout persons whose religious interest is predominantly ethical and social who seem to have no difficulty in resolving the theological issue into a semantic one. They have some understanding of religious experience but are not easily reached by doctrine.

A Church-State Issue

There is another aspect of this matter, however, that is more substantial in the present context. It seems not to have occurred to theological anti-Communists that to wage political war on Communism on the ground that it is atheistic is to bring a religious issue into a state matter. The most orthodox of us would hardly think of campaigning against a candidate for office on the ground that he was, let us say, like Jefferson and some of the other founding fathers, a deist rather than a theist. In making up our own minds how to vote we may be guided by any reason or bias, but we would not regard a religious test as establishing a candidate's superiority in terms of citizenship. To be sure, this may be a criticism of religion, as practiced, but the point is that in a secular state and in a world made up largely of secular states we can hardly expect to influence a person's political standing by attacking him on religious grounds. This is the old doctrine of separation between church and state projected on a global canvas. Combining it with the record of experience in the crusade against Communism, where do we come out? In the light of the meager results that we have witnessed of the sustained barrage against atheistic Communism is such a strategy rational or consistent?

Moreover, however we may interpret it or feel about it, the fact is that some of the most ardent defenders of democracy and resolute foes of totalitarianism in America are unready to commit themselves to a theistic position. It is doubtless due in part to this fact that the U. S. Constitution forbids any test of religious belief as qualifying citizens for public service. Such a test, however significant religiously, is, as a matter of public policy, regarded as not directly relevant to qualification for useful citizenship in a pluralist society.

The Essence of the Matter

The basic issue, then, from an ethical standpoint, would seem to be one of over-all policy: Is Communism's challenge to be met by a strategy that assumes an eventual military showdown—by one that deliberately risks all-out war? Or by competition in production, trade, diplomacy, and propaganda, as Premier Khrushchev proposes? In a word, shall we accept a warlike relationship as normative for an indefinite period—as a way of life for nations ideologically opposed—or shall we seek a *modus vivendi?*

Admittedly, there are hazards in either course, but, repugnant as the alternatives offered by the Soviet Union usually are, it is hardly possible to find a rational and moral basis for rejecting outright the challenge of the Soviet Union to substitute for the ordeal of war economic competition in an open market. The issue here is not one of Communist sincerity or trustworthiness. A cold war, as well as a hot war—and we have noted that Communism considers itself always engaged in one or the other—involves many a breach of peacetime ethics as the mutual practice of espionage on a big scale has now made startlingly clear. We face "a condition, and not a theory," and must decide between the alternatives offered.

Economic Competition Instead of War

Among the specific elements of what I have called a valid strategy, the economic front claims first attention. Competition in economic development and foreign trade admittedly involves an element of venture, but it must be measured against the hazard that is implicit in ultimate reliance upon force—with the prospect of immeasurable destruction.

To be sure, the economic competition to which Communism is challenging us is not likely to be, at the outset at least, a "gentlemen's affair." The director of one of our great research organizations has said: "The collision ahead between U.S. and Soviet aims (not armies, note) will loom over a thousand decisions yet to be made. It may seem a relatively small matter when Russian dumping of aluminum forces down U.S. and Canadian aluminum prices, but the day is not far when business decisions in American cities will have to be made with a constant eye on Moscow." Indeed, competition in business and industry within one nation is itself a process which has to be in greater or less degree policed by government in order to prevent it from becoming intolerably predatory and destructive, but the crudest kind of economic competition is infinitely preferable to a competitive race in the production of "ultimate" weapons of war. From a Christian viewpoint the possibility may not be excluded that the dynamism of Russia may become more benign—no longer an intolerable outward thrust of naked power. Indeed, this is to be expected in the case of any movement that has a crusading aspect. The *élan* weakens as the years pass. Aging, in a cause or an individual life, has a melancholy aspect from which it has to be redeemed by faith and works. In this particular case there is excellent reason to believe that the most potent factor in shaping the future of the Soviet Union will be the political environment in which it finds itself.

However, at the risk of incurring criticism I am constrained to say that the outcome to be expected or hoped for is not a new Russia fashioned in the image of the West. Running through our whole inquiry has been a sense of the unforeseen, the unpredictable. If victory over Communism, in the sense of conquest, is what we are after, the aim is of doubtful validity and questionable realizability. It may even be said that the most essential element in meeting the crisis of Western civilization now looming ahead of us is the abandonment of a definite blueprint of the "right" kind of social order. Why is it so hard for human beings to accept the idea that norms of living are not static, but always undergoing modification? Rubbing our eyes, we have awakened to the fact that theories we thought ridiculous now demand a testing. Unless we are willing to face the fact of continuous change in the patterns of production and exchange and the distribution of the product of industry, we have disqualified ourselves for the race that is to be run.

Is it not curious that the vast changes that have already come about in our capitalist system have not convinced all defenders of free enterprise that that term never defined a fixed pattern of procedures, but a quality to be valued and preserved? The leaders of American industry a generation ago, if they could be reanimated and could survey the present scene, would no doubt exclaim, "All is lost." Even among our contemporaries there is much dismal foreboding.

Former Vice-president Richard Nixon once called upon the country to accept Premier Khrushchev's challenge to substitute economic competition for military competition. This is one of Khrushchev's utterances that unquestionably makes sense, and the challenge should be accepted, not for the sake of international courtesy, which is now in short supply, but in the interest of sanity.

Increase East-West Trade

All of a piece with economic growth, in accord with a sound coexistence principle, is the unhampered extension of trade. Theoretical economists have for generations favored free trade, but practical considerations make certain controls unavoidable, particularly in wartime. It would, however, probably surprise most Americans to know the extent of the readiness of business leaders in this country to trade with Communist countries when approval by Washington is forthcoming. During the first half of 1959 American exports to Eastern Europe amounted to nearly 29,000,000 dollars, but exports to Poland accounted for most of it. During that period our imports from Eastern Europe were over 40,000,000, of which more than 23,000,000 came from Poland. These figures represent a small volume by comparison with that of Anglo-Soviet trade.

A curious anomaly is apparent here. Industrial and business leaders, who have most at stake, in material terms, in the East-West struggle and who are usually most vocal in their opposition to Communism, seem to take a more pragmatic view of trade with the Communist bloc than do our most vocal statesmen. A rationale for this attitude is tersely put in a publication of the American Management Association:

> If the political leaders of the world are able to reach some sort of agreement, the Soviet threat will become commercial instead of military. It will be up to us in the West to continue to offer a better way of life to the peoples of the world than do the Communists. In the future, it would seem, international problems between the East and the West will center upon ideological competition for the satisfaction of man's spiritual needs and upon commercial competition for the satisfaction of man's physical needs.[10]

This means, of course, that the cold war will continue in a clash of ideas, a prospect that is quite realistic. There is no end to this low-temperature war in sight. The point is that the combatants in such warfare can "live to fight another day!"

Because of their source and their immediate relevance to our subject in what is certainly one of its most crucial aspects, I am making reference to three other articles in this illuminating document issued by the American Management Association. The first is an extraordinarily blunt statement on the writer's experience in U.S.-Soviet trade. The following is a brief excerpt:

> I am still of the opinion that the basic aim of Soviet foreign policy is to persist in political and economic aggression for the purpose of world domination. On the other hand, I am inclined to agree with Mr. Khrushchev that our own foreign policy is cockeyed, in that we failed to recognize the Soviets for 16 years but had a thriving business with them, then recognized them and gradually choked the business to death. We have traded with them in the past without in any way endangering ourselves, and we can do it again. I see nothing to gain by sticking our heads in the sand and refusing to see what is there. The Soviets are progressing rapidly, and they will be tough competitors. . . .
>
> Actually, I rate the Communist threat as a proper challenge. Discontent, ignorance, and poverty make conquest easy for promising political

[10] J. B. Scott, "The Anglo-Soviet Five-Year Trade Agreement: Its Background, Content, and Implications," *Aspects of East-West Trade*, AMA Management Report No. 45. New York: American Management Association (1960), p. 30. Used by permission.

opportunists, whether they use Marxism or any other propaganda. If we do, in fact, have a better system—and I am absolutely certain that we do—then we had better be able to stand up and take it. I believe that we have a real need to "come alive," and that if we continue along our present path we will certainly lose out in the face of changing world conditions.[11]

Another bit of testimony is given on behalf of the chemical industry:

The world is now divided into two huge economic blocs politically isolated from each other. While each of these blocs seems to be working out its own economic problems internally with some degree of success, these political barriers are probably, in the last analysis, economically unsound. As the populations of the world increase, and as the so-called "underdeveloped" areas of the world become more highly developed and thus require more and more of the goods of modern economy, there will be increasing pressure to break down these artificial political barriers. This kind of pressure could, of course, bring about a war, but the cost of war is now so great than any aggressor would probably destroy the industrial and economic objectives he set out to achieve.

In short, it is my personal opinion that everyone in the East and the West should work toward a normal world economy.[12]

Finally, the reader is urged to note a more detailed statement of the case for U.S.-Soviet trade:

In June 1958 Premier Khrushchev made what seems to me to be a serious proposal to President Eisenhower that the governments of the two countries enter into a trade agreement. . . . He stressed that he did not have in mind trade in armaments or plant equipment for military production. . . . In return, he proposed, the Soviet Union could deliver such commodities as manganese and chromium ores, ferrous alloys, platinum, palladium, asbestos, potassium salts, lumber, cellulose and paper products, certain chemical products, furs, and possibly iron ore, as well as a number of types of modern machinery and equipment

[11] Robert C. Lee, "Trading with the Soviets: One American's Experiences from 1925 to 1960," *ibid.*, p. 58.

[12] Cleveland Lane, "The U. S. Chemical Industry's Views on Trade with the Soviets," *ibid.*, p. 67.

which, he said, might be of interest to American firms. . . .

It was a mistake, in my opinion, for the President to reject this proposal on the ground that the Soviet Union should approach private firms if it wants to develop a larger volume of trade with this country. In the first place, it is difficult for the Soviet Union to establish commercial relations with American exporters because of the complexities of our export-licensing system: There is never complete assurance that an export license will be granted or, if granted, that it will not be revoked. In the second place, if we do business with the Soviet Union on the basis of such a trade agreement—as almost all the Western European countries do—we can insure that it is advantageous to this country as a whole and not merely to the Russians.[12]

The writer then lists a number of stipulations which such a trade agreement should embody by way of protecting our national interest, after which he comments:

We cannot discuss Mr. Khrushchev's proposals as "mere propaganda." To declare, as our Government officials have repeatedly done, that the Russians are really interested only in buying strategic goods or in obtaining huge credits, and that they really have nothing to sell us, is no answer to a concrete proposal to exchange peaceful products. If it is true that the offer is a mere bluff, then the best answer is to call it; if it is not a bluff, then the best answer is still to put down our chips.[14]

Cultural Interchange

Cultural interchange between East and West among scholars and students in various disciplines, with maximum freedom of travel, is of incalculable importance. This judgment rests on experience, particularly in scientific collaboration and with the student-exchange program. It is quite as true with respect to students from Asia and Africa, where ideology is not frozen.

Long-range plans for such interchange on a large scale may well prove to be the most potent factor in creating the intellectual and spiritual conditions of international peace and amity. It would be in some sense a venture of faith on our part as far as

[13] Harold J. Berman, "Negotiating Commercial Transactions with Soviet Customers," *ibid.*, pp. 73-74.
[14] *Ibid.*, p. 75.

Communist-bloc nations are concerned, since the obstacles to be overcome are more numerous in the Communist sphere. But democracy itself is a venture of faith. The results of existing exchange programs give abundant reason to think that increased personal contacts between American citizens and those of countries under Communist regimes can be directly productive of both understanding and good will. Members of the Christian churches should see at once the common elements between such a cultural enterprise and the newer type missionary activity which aims at mutual understanding, appreciation, and respect.

It has been pointed out, however, that where student-exchange programs are not carefully planned, where guidance is not given to the prospective visiting student, and where adequate preparation is not made by the institutions concerned, the net results may be anything but gratifying. Yet well-conceived, well-sponsored, and wisely carried-through exchange plans promise very large results in the way of international peace and good will and co-operation among peoples. It has been noted again and again by travelers that the Russian people, when greeted by American tourists, exhibit a bewildered and wistful friendliness toward these strangers against whom they have been officially warned.

"Foreign Aid"

There must be, at long last, what a previous administration proposed as a "bold new program," looking toward the development of natural resources and the promotion of technological advance among the underdeveloped countries of the world. There are, for a nation whose economic resources are growing as rapidly as they are in America, continually widening avenues for trade and for investment, motivated not merely by altruism but by a profound sense of mutual interest. Economic prosperity is a multilateral matter. If obstacles to trade are removed economic factors will themselves dictate a flow of high economic potential from the richer to the poorer countries to the advantage of both, because the continuous discovery and development of new sources of wealth are a basic form of economic activity. There are difficulties in the way, to be sure; we are greatly concerned about economic recession and the disturbing balance of payments, but these are not unmanageable.

To the greatest possible extent these programs involving investment and technical assistance should be separated from programs of military defense. It is obvious that trade and investment cannot and should not be wholly independent of the national defense, but it is important that the motivation behind them should be convincingly independent of the pursuit of military advantage.

Such considerations must not be taken for sentimentality. Preferential aid to allies in a momentous struggle should of course be taken for granted. Within limits, foreign aid inescapably becomes an instrument of military policy. The great prototype of such undertakings—the Marshall Plan—was frankly linked to national policy, and made history. In that instance, however, mutual involvement of sending and receiving countries was so momentous that the enterprise justified itself beyond question. The Marshall Plan became historic because it embodied the purpose expressed in words that General George C. Marshall spoke when he anounced it: "Our policy is directed not against any country or doctrine but against hunger, poverty, desperation and chaos. Its purpose should be the revival of a working economy in the world so as to permit the emergence of political and social conditions in which free institutions can exist." What should give us concern in all our aid programs is that they should not be designed to purchase adherence to a bloc of which the United States is the power center, to combat neutralism, or to win gratitude.

We have heard much in this connection of the proverbial dislike that benevolence engenders in the recipient. The only substance in such assertions inheres, not in the act of bestowal, but in the inappropriate attitudes which prompt it and which "show through." Again, we are dealing here not just with benevolence, but with statesmanship.

There is a more fundamental aspect of this subject, however. The concept itself of foreign aid is defective. Here is an excellent example of what I tried to say earlier about the national interest. Good international relations, like good personal relations, flow from a sense of mutual involvement. Certainly Christianity can settle for nothing less. We see peoples suffering hardship and privation, and we say, "While they are in prison we are not free."

The long-term needs are for capital and technical assistance. There is appalling immediate need for sustenance. The *Economic World* reported in the summer of 1960:

> More than half of the entire population of the non-Communist world are living today in almost unbelievably miserable conditions. Theirs is a constant struggle against incredibly low incomes, against hunger, disease, illiteracy. To create the necessary momentum to generate their own savings to invest for development, they must have outside help— investment, capital and technical assistance.
>
> These are the people who are searching for economic and social progress as a means to achieve individual and national freedom. This is the "Revolution of Rising Expectations." [15]

What must these millions say to each other when they read of our mountainous food surpluses?

National Defense

This study is not concerned with the critical technical problems of military defense. That issues of life and death for the human race should go undecided because equally qualified experts cannot agree is one of the most grievous facts of our time. There are aspects of military defense, however, that inevitably concern us here.

One of these is closely related to the preceding topic—which accounts for the sequence. The problem of financing the basic needs of peoples suffering chronic want cannot fail to bring into painful awareness our fabulous expenditures for defense. In a publication received as these pages were written, *A World Without War*, Walter Millis wrote:

[15] August-September, 1960. Committee for International Economic Growth, Washington 6, D. C.

A VITAL ENCOUNTER: CHRISTIANITY AND COMMUNISM

We are already alarmed by the problem of doing without the 10 per cent or so of our national production that we now pour down the drain of military preparedness. . . . We now dump some $50 billions' worth a year of weaponry and military organization into the maintenance of international order, without expectation of financial return. Economically, this is a dead loss. But if we are already "subsidizing" or underwriting world order in these amounts, there seems to be no reason why we should not continue doing so in other forms, much more efficient for the purpose. And there is much reason to think that we shall have to do so. The tendencies toward rationalization, planning, social rather than merely financial cost-accounting, which we see marching so imperiously forward within our own domestic economy, are equally imperious in the international world, and organized war is simply an obstruction to them, not a necessary support for them.[16]

The abolition of war is an end in itself and the ethical mandate to achieve it needs no extraneous support. But the consummation of this task and relief of human want everywhere in the world may well turn out to be the obverse and reverse sides of one mission of emancipation.

By the same token, disarmament is in the last analysis not so much a means to world peace as the fruit of a successful effort to remove the incentives to military conquest—in a word, to paralyze the will to war. This is not to detract from the importance of what the experts are doing to effect a breakthrough in the mountain of apparatus of destruction that compulsive terror has piled in humanity's path. The danger of a trigger-finger nuclear war, while probably not so great as many fear, is enough to warrant ceaseless efforts to ban these barbaric inventions—as the effects of lethal fallout are enough to impel all the nuclear powers to find a way to put an end to nuclear testing.

It should also be said that there is a certain adolescent vanity behind the pressures put upon our government to spend and spend on defense, regardless of the strain upon our economic system. No matter how unholy some of the incentives to produce profits may be, a breakdown of the economy under the weight of

[16] Center for the Study of Democratic Institutions, Santa Barbara, California (1961). Used by permission.

defense costs is possible and the time may conceivably come when such waste must have a stop.

"Quiet Diplomacy"

We are now hearing about "quiet diplomacy," both by way of reaction to the effort to achieve Woodrow Wilson's goal of "open covenants openly arrived at" and by way of protest against the Soviet pattern of diplomacy, which makes it in large part an exercise in high-powered propaganda. Two observations are in order here.

First, it has long been increasingly apparent that the Wilsonian slogan can be carried too far. Effective diplomacy directed at ironing out disputes between governments cannot be conducted in a goldfish bowl. Off-the-record proceedings are salutary and indeed necessary when crucial and delicate matters are under consideration. If unpublicized exploration does not precede public commitment the results may range from futility to disaster. As one prominent political scientist has put it, "If diplomats have to carry out their missions in front of a television audience they will, perforce, be actors first and diplomats only second. In fact, diplomacy will become play-acting, which is not diplomacy at all.[17] "Summitry" may be an excellent climax of diplomacy, but its utility is sharply limited. (An experienced ecclesiastical administrator should have no difficulty in assimilating this fact.) The evil in secret diplomacy results from secret agreements and "understandings" which the peoples concerned have a right to know about and perhaps to ratify or reject.

Secondly, even when this principle is recognized, the fact must be reckoned with that present-day diplomacy is qualitatively different from the traditional type in that it involves not only adjustment and accommodation, but ideological confrontation. Communist preference for summit conferences and public debates, amply televised and beamed to all the world, is not merely an aspect of clever trickery: It reflects the fact that the Communists are not primarily trying to convince or persuade diplo-

[17] Louis J. Halle, "The Case for Quiet Diplomacy," The New York *Times Magazine* (September 11, 1960).

mats, but to sell something to the peoples of the world who are eagerly tuning in—the underprivileged, and especially the un-committed. This is a stubborn fact of our revolutionary era. We must expect that propaganda will continue to be an aspect of diplomacy during the foreseeable future.

Walter Lippmann has put the essence of the matter in admir-ably concise form: "The great task of quiet diplomacy is to work out ways and means of keeping the critical questions—Laos, the Congo, Algeria, Cuba—from reaching the point of irreparable decision." [18]

The U.S. and the UN

At long last we in the United States seem to have discovered the stake we have in the United Nations. Too many of our American citizens have had a rather supercilious attitude toward the organization, regarding it as a rather extravagant and perhaps ill-conceived benevolent enterprise. It has cost the United States a lot of money and has been systematically hampered by the Soviet Union. The saving consideration, with those who have given at least half-hearted support to the UN has been the fact that the United States has been able to line up enough pro-Western support to defeat Communist efforts to subvert the pur-poses of the organization. Hence our heavy contributions to its budget could be viewed as payments on a national insurance policy.

Now, however, some startling developments have occurred. The political stock of the United States has been going down in the world market. This is said not by way of reviving campaign charges—or arguments in rebuttal—about prestige. Be that mat-ter as it may, the important fact is that for one or another reason nations that had been wont to follow the lead of the United States began to set their courses independently—or under other influence. They found their national interest pointing in a different direction. The Western bloc began to lose its coherence and its leadership was no longer secure. Even in Latin America

[18] New York *Herald Tribune* (January 10, 1961).

political restiveness was evident on the diplomatic front. These developments had reverberations in the United Nations.

All this came about gradually—in terms of the political tempo of our time. In 1960, however, an event of seismic proportions occurred: The admission to the UN of a group of new national states whose orientation to the East-West struggle was unpredictable, even in the minds of their precariously poised leaders. The organization, which at its birth had fifty-one members—thirty-two of them from Western Europe and the Americas—now has ninety-nine members, fifty-four of them belonging to what is called the Afro-Asian bloc.

Thus, within a relatively short period the United States found itself shorn of its dominance in the United Nations, and even unsure of its ability to prevent actions instigated by the Communist bloc which Washington would regard as highly undesirable and perhaps ominous. This does not mean, of course, that the Afro-Asian group is really a "bloc" in the sense in which that may be said of the nations in the Communist orbit. Indeed, the evidence that the members of this group will, for the most part, not become satellites is at this moment the chief hope of the West. By the same token, however, the new configuration of power units means for the United States that while our government can no longer count on its ability to chart the course of the United Nations, neither can it conduct its foreign relations unilaterally. The United States now needs the United Nations as the United Nations has from its inception needed the United States.[19] It might even be said that the less power we have to guide its policy the greater our need of the organization will be.

At this moment the Soviet Union, thoroughly hostile to the administration of the United Nations, seems bent on crippling the organization. Yet it would be a grievous error to treat this situation as an impasse. In the present precarious state of international relations to accept any event, any situation, as a terminal

---

[19] Since this sentence was written I have been struck by the way it conforms to the statement made by James J. Wadsworth at the time he turned over his office at the UN to his successor, Adlai E. Stevenson. He said that "the United States needs the United Nations just as much, if not more, than the United Nations needs the United States."

point in the search for a basis of durable peace would be to invite disaster. There is good reason to believe that the Kremlin is acutely aware of this. It is even possible that the fantastic behavior of Premier Khrushchev and the seemingly illogical gyrations of Soviet foreign policy have been dictated by a felt necessity to combine a convincing belligerency with an unfailing agility in keeping out of war. (Perhaps "brinkmanship" is really of Russian origin!)

In any case, Wadsworth, after serving for eight years as a U. S. delegate to the United Nations—and bearing the brunt of some of the Soviet Union's most truculent attacks, could say, "I think generally, by and large, that the Russian Government has every intention of living up to any agreement they may make from the standpoint of nuclear tests or the larger areas of disarmament." Taken together with concessions the Soviet government has made in the course of the negotiations on nuclear testing, this "voice of experience" strongly suggests that the possibilities of agreement have not been exhausted.

Moreover, it must be recognized that the Soviet revolt in the United Nations was against a policy that, while sound and statesmanlike from our point of view, did constitute a departure from the original conception of the United Nations. That is to say, from the definitely limited role of carrying out purposes indicated by consensus—in major matters a consensus of five great powers—the Director-General of the organization has steered it, under the impact of grave crises, into a new role, that of safeguarding the weaker neutral nations from becoming embroiled in the cold war. Russia's effort to thwart this move is reactionary and deplorable, but it is not exactly sabotage—and may not be, in intent, totally destructive.

It is in this context that the issue of admitting Communist China to the United Nations should be weighed. The question is not one of legal claim or moral right. If the decision is to be based on premises of this sort it may well be that a negative conclusion is foregone. No, the question is not one of individual or national guilt; it is whether or not the principle of universality of membership is essential to the performance of the functions of the United

Nations. The Arden House Conference in January, 1961, summed it up this way:

> We regard it as desirable that the government of the People's Republic of China be drawn into fuller participation in the international community, leading to regularization of its diplomatic relations with other countries, including the United States, participation in the work and responsibilities of the United Nations, and participation in present efforts to achieve international agreement on a suspension of nuclear testing and steps toward reduction and control of armaments. We reaffirm our support for the independence of Taiwan.[20]

I wish to make it unmistakably clear that nothing in the text of this volume is intended as a defense of or argument for a particular policy concerning the relations between the United States and Red China or the policy of our government with respect to admission of the latter to the United Nations. It is possible to present a strong rationale for a settlement of the China issue which is more in line with the palpable political realities of the Far-Eastern situation, while at the same time holding, as such liberals as Adlai Stevenson and Senator Paul H. Douglas have done, that Red China is still in a position of being disqualified for participation in the UN. Likewise one may recognize and deplore the anomaly in the relation of Nationalist China to the whole political complex of the Far East while at the same time insisting that commitments long ago made by the United States cannot be disregarded without violence to our national conscience.

In other words, it is possible to make an impressive case for each of two wholly contrary policies. This appears to be the reason for the stalemate we are now witnessing. That the present status of China in international affairs can be permanently maintained is a proposition hard to defend.

An Unprecedented Educational Task

Soviet Russia has done innumerable bad things and many stupid things. No one can know the price she is paying for her

---

[20] New York *Times* (January 16, 1961), reporting on conference of a group of prominent scientists, business men, educators and technicians.

wanton dissipation of an enormous reservoir of goodwill—perhaps naïve goodwill—in the West when World War II came to an end. It is hard to understand how intelligent people can defend the banalities of Russian propaganda and the elaborate distortion of facts unblushingly perpetrated on all who can be misled or intimidated by such tactics. Despite all this, however, the Soviet Union has found ways to deploy material and personal resources for the creation of an educational system of vast scope and efficiency. In some respects it puts ours to shame. The disproportionate emphasis on the physical sciences is to be deplored, though it can be understood as an effort to build up national prestige and instruments of national power. Yet there is abundant evidence in Russia of eager interest in the humanities and the arts.

The main point of these comments is that the Soviet Union is putting forth tremendous efforts to create a new culture and a new personality type in keeping with Communist ideals and aims. The program has, of course, a terrifying aspect because of its totalitarian character. As Lenin said, "In the field of people's education the Communist Party sets itself the aim of concluding the task begun by the October Revolution of 1917 of converting the school from a weapon for the class domination of the bourgeoisie into a weapon for the destruction of this domination, as well as for the complete destruction of the division of society into classes. The school must become a weapon of the dictatorship of the proletariat." [21]

This is conditioning with a vengeance, and that is a bad word in the American educator's vocabulary. It needs to be remembered, however, that all good education has in an important sense a conditioning function. It sets the stage, so to speak, for a way of life—a system of values and a pattern of behavior—acceptable to the culture. Education in the West should be frankly aimed at cultivation of the democratic way of life and should pursue that end unremittingly. Such a program should not be confused with authoritarian indoctrination.

[21] Quoted by George S. Counts, *The Challenge of Soviet Education, op. cit.,* p. 47.

The moral of all this is that the West—and in particular the United States of America—has an educational responsibility corresponding to that which the Soviet Union and Communist China have taken upon themselves. They are frank about their purpose to change the nature of man and of society. The United States, prevailingly Christian and democratic in profession, has a heritage that includes these aims, albeit on a vastly different model. It is doubtful if any chapter of human history records the coexistence of two great movements so sharply in contrast philosophically and ethically and so similar in *avowed* ultimate purposes for man and society. In contemplating them one is reminded of H. G. Wells' often quoted statement concerning human destiny as the outcome of a race between education and disaster. In terms of magnitude of effort, precision of aim, and distance run toward the chosen goal, the Soviet Union is far ahead of us. If we cannot do a better job of implementing our avowed purposes than we are now doing, the outlook is not bright.

One aspect of this educational task is teaching with respect to Communism itself. The conventional negative attitude toward it is politically fatuous and morally wrong. In an illuminating article on this subject in *The Yardstick,* a news feature of the National Catholic Welfare Conference, late in 1960 Monsignor George G. Higgins, its scholarly editor, wrote: "The District of Columbia School Board announced recently that a guide for teaching sixth graders the truth about Communism and for acquainting them with the difference between Communism and the American system will be available to District teachers for the first time this year."

This project was commended as laudable, but the editor added:

The members of the District School Board, however, will probably be subjected to a certain amount of criticism for adopting this course of studies. They may be told, for example, that in offering such a course to immature students they are running the risk of unwittingly indoctrinating some of them in Communism.

In my judgment, if there is any such risk involved, it is of negligible proportions and can easily be guarded against with a minimum of care on the part of teachers and administrators. Moreover, it is not to be compared with the much greater risk which our schools would be running if they were to ignore the subject of Communism completely.[22]

It is gratifying to know that guided study is being initiated in this area, including study of the Russian language.

Of vital importance is a clear understanding that there are various forms of democratic socialism which cannot be equated with Communism. It is true, of course, that those who oppose *any* increase in power on the part of the state may plausibly contend that any movement in that direction may be a prelude to measures that look in the direction of the omnicompetent state. But certainly many revolutionary movements now stirring the world have more in common with the democratic social tradition of the West than they have with international Communism. India is the foremost example of a nation committed to the Western democratic tradition apparently bent on following a national policy which is more accurately labeled socialism than capitalism, though far removed from Communism in form and, so to speak, in political stance. Incidentally, the term "committed" suffers violence when used merely to designate an orientation toward the conflict between East and West rather than toward a total way of life. It is not strange that the leaders of a people finding itself surrounded and conditioned by competing nationalisms should be constrained to say "a plague on both your houses." Such a tendency is fostered by what has been called "hypertrophy of nationalism," which in great and small nations alike tends to displace political philosophy and ideology in the struggle for power and status.

"Person-to-Person"

This book embodies an attempt to clarify in some measure the religious, political, and social issues raised by the encounter between Communism and our Western—particularly our American—ideals and institutions, presupposing as they do the validity of a value system derived in large part from the biblical tradition. These issues are, in the first instance and predominantly, politi-

[22] Used by permission.

cal and economic because those are the areas in which national interests are challenged and national policies are evolved which affect the lives and destinies of whole populations. The churches, however, are involved on two fronts, so to speak, because they have inherited the apostolic commission to "go into all the world" carrying the gospel to persons, and at the same time they recognize a certain responsibility to mold the conscience of the national community with respect to international relations. Thus organized religion has two complementary missions which need to be brought into a working relationship vis-à-vis international Communism.

We noted earlier that Christian missionary strategy has achieved much in this direction in relation to non-Christian religions, but the impact of Communism upon Christianity is intrinsically different from that resulting from the Christian encounter with other world religions, even with Islam. Communist doctrine is negative toward all theistic concepts and all forms of religious worship, because these are deemed subversive of the Communist movement. Christians can, and do, work with Jews, with Hindus, with Buddhists, and with Muslims toward mutually desired ethical and spiritual ends, and with mutual respect.

In contrast to this, co-operation between Christians and Communists cannot without much difficulty and hazard take place except in a limited secular area, and even there only precariously, because their philosophies and ethical systems are felt to be intrinsically antagonistic, each a menace to the other. For the same reason a person-to-person Christian-Communist encounter— a reciprocal "soul-winning" effort—tends to be an enterprise in "radical displacement" which leaves the person who is won over "deracinated" culturally and perhaps spiritually up-rooted.

That conversions of Communists to Christianity occur is definitely attested, but they seem to be relatively few. Conversely, conversions from Christianity to Communism seldom, if ever, occur. What does occasionally happen is that a Christian becomes convinced that Communism actually is, in some significant sense, an expression of authentic Christian concerns. To the extent that he embraces Communism he regards it as a social, this-worldly projection of Christian ethics into the existential human situation. The disillusionment that often follows comes in the form of discovery that the correspondence between Christianity and the revolutionary secular faith may be all too superficial. The point here is that such a person regards himself as still a Christian— a more consistent one than before.

It may be a startling thing to say, but I cannot see how sincere, disciplined Communists—the kind missionaries write about with a sort of baffled admiration—can be "evangelized" by a traditional approach. With those who are not sincere, who are trafficking in power, or otherwise pursuing their own advantage, the problem is of course wholly different. They are, like all "sinners," in need of a change of heart. But the dedicated Communist is likely to be won to the Christian faith only by finding his way into a dedicated community, one that has heroically taken up the challenge of Communism in the spirit of Christ and is working at its task in authentic Christian fashion.

Moreover, it is safe to assume that relatively few of the citizens of the Soviet Union and Red China, to say nothing of smaller nations in the Communist bloc, are fully indoctrinated, "dyed-in-the-wool" Communists. The degree of their susceptibility to a Christian appeal is indeterminate.

No matter how many frustrations and disillusionments are experienced by Christians who make a personal appeal to Communists, it would be contrary to the very genius of Christianity to assume that such efforts must be hopeless. One of the best-known and most highly regarded Christian leaders in America wrote in this connection:

As to the way in which the churches or church-related agencies might act in relation to Communists, I would hope that Christians would take an active lead in getting to know some of the Communists of their communities and would invite them to their homes and to their churches. From the experience that I have had, they would not be over-run by responses, but at least the Communists would have evidence of the church's interest in them as human beings instead of being afraid of them as Communists.

180

Setting Our Own House in Order

We in the United States are under a heavy moral obligation to rid our national life of those blots—with respect to race relations, crime, delinquency, racketeering, and the like—which foreign critics are able to cite with devastating effect on our national reputation. Prestige is not the right word here. Moral reputation is more important than prestige, of which so much was heard in the presidential campaign of 1960.

There is a mischievous sentiment abroad to the effect that it is somehow disloyal to the United States to focus attention on these national faults. The contrary is true. Self-criticism enhances the stature of a nation as well as of an individual. The effort here proposed, however, calls for a degree of national humility which we have never yet achieved. The facts about our domestic faults and failings are well known abroad—and exaggerated. A demonstration that we are aware of them, that we are grievously concerned over them, and are determined to take effective action to end them cannot fail to increase respect for the United States throughout the world.

Our task, however, is much more than house cleaning. We have habituated ourselves to a defensive stance—protecting the American way of life as something ultimate in terms of political and social theory and practice. We are right concerning the American idea, immortalized by Lincoln at Gettysburg, but the testing of our national viability of which he spoke that day is still in process. As the Communist nations are striving to build what they call socialism, we are still laboring to build democracy. This discussion is sharpened up by a statement that has just come to my desk concerning the nature of the democratic ideal and the responsibility that its acceptance imposes:

Democracy does not expect men to be angels; but it does not propose to treat them, therefore, as sheep. The great wager on which it stakes its destiny is that the imperfectible individual is improvable. And it believes that the best way to improve him is to let him improve himself, to give him as much responsibility as possible for his own destiny and for the destiny of the community to which he belongs. Democratic governments have been prepared to take positive steps to free the individual from avoidable handicaps so that he can run the race on fair terms with others. They are committed today to providing all individuals with the basic forms of economic security that are essential to a decent life. But their objective is not to produce tame, well-tended men and women who are easy to harness to a master plan. Their objective is to release the powers of individuals and to turn loose the flow of human initiative.

There is, therefore, a kind of inner tension that is perennially present in the democratic way of life. A democracy must balance its faith in the potentialities of the individual against its realistic appraisal of his capacities for judgment and responsible behavior.[23]

The most effective way to combat the evils we find in Communism is to labor ceaselessly to bring this democratic ideal to fruition.

In bringing this report to a close I am making use of some impressive words written by Dean John C. Bennett of Union Theological Seminary in his book, *Christians and the State*. Referring to the "terrible urgency" of the international situation he wrote:

Human existence on earth is at stake. Also at stake is the freedom of many nations from at least temporary totalitarian domination. Is there any reality harder to live with than the fact that at the very time when the weapons of war threaten mutual annihilation, the moral and spiritual split within humanity has become deepest? Because of this split, it is difficult to arrive at any accord that might make possible reduction and control of armaments and the development of a United Nations strong enough to restrain any recalcitrant great power. . . . This confusing situation makes a direct approach by western Christians as Christians to the problem of the moral and spiritual split almost as difficult as the approach of western statesmen to the political conflict.[24]

Further on he says: "The hope for the future lies not in victory over Communism in Russia or China, but in the changes in Communism which come with a new generation that is more

[23] From: *The Power of the Democratic Idea*, Copyright © Rockefeller Brothers Fund, Inc. Reprinted by permission of Doubleday and Company, Inc.

[24] New York: Charles Scribner's Sons, 1958, p. 164. Used by permission.

concerned about the building of their own society than with ideology or world-revolution." [25]

The "vital encounter," which is too often mistakenly thought of as primarily military, is a trial of the moral fiber and spiritual insight of nations, institutions, and persons whose interests, both real and fancied, have set them in opposing array. In such a conflict there can be no worthwhile victory without mutual cleansing and enrichment of the human spirit.

[25] *Ibid.,* p. 190.

INDEX

Acton, Lord, 152
Adams, J. Donald, 66
Afghanistan, 21
Africa
  Communism in, 20
  students to U.S. from, 166
Alexius, Patriarch, 75
Almond, Gabriel, quoted, 49, 65
American League Against War and
  Fascism (for Peace and Free-
  dom), 91
American Management Association,
  quoted, 164-65
Amoy University, 89
Anderson, Paul B., quoted, 113-14
Anti-colonialism, 52-55
Anti-Communism, 22, 24-25, 93, 95,
  96, 157-60
Anti-foreign foreigners, 69
Antireligious campaign, 67-68, 105-
  6, 107, 113
Apostles of Revolution (Nomad),
  quoted, 44
Arden House Conference, quoted,
  175
Argentina, Communism in, 21, 25,
  87
Art, Christian, 108-9
Asia
  Communism in, 20-21
  students to U.S. from, 166
  see also China
Atheism, 107, 109, 113, 120, 159-60
Atomic bomb, 104
Authoritarianism, appeal of, 75-76

Bakunin, Mikhail, 30, 32, 33
Balance-of-power formula, 132
Baptists, in U.S.S.R., 111, 112, 113
Barth, Karl, quoted, 124-25
Belgium, Communism in, 19
Bennett, John C., quoted, 104, 182-
  83
Berdyaev, quoted, 34, 35
Berlin crisis, 14
Berliner, Joseph S., quoted, 72-73
Beveridge, Albert J., quoted, 36
Bolshevism, 28, 33, 34, 35
Boris, Archbishop, 111

Bourgeoisie, 38
Brainwashing, 48
Brazil, 21
Bricker Amendment, 133
Browder, Earl, quoted, 114-15
Buchanan, James, quoted, 143
Buddhism, 118

Camus, Albert, 66
Cantril, Hadley, quoted, 57, 58, 70-
  72
Capitalism, 40, 42, 44, 163
  as American way of life, 55
  changes in, 46,
  competition of Communism and,
    17, 129, 130, 131, 161-63
  evils of, 67, 124
  international aspect of, 79
  struggle against, 80
  view of, as unhealthy, 71
Caracas Declaration, 138
Castro, Fidel, 14, 22
"Catechism of a Revolutionist," 30-
  32
Catholic Church, 35, 99
  in China, 119
  Communist members of, 57-58,
    59, 61, 160
  and Communist Party in U.S.,
    114-15
  two concepts of, 57-58
  use of, in Communist approach,
    87
  and worker priests, 62-64
Centralism
  Communist principle of, 95
  democratic, 38
CGIL (Italian labor union), 19, 60
Chambers, Whittaker, quoted, 69-
  70
China Communist
  authenticity of regime in, 43
  background for, 67-69
  break of, with past, 29
  communes in, 47
  conflict of, with U.S.S.R., 40, 41
  continuing problems in, 154
  missionary approach in, 56-57, 86-
    87, 88-89

China Communists—*cont'd*
Muslims in, 117
population in, 46-47
question of admission of, to
United Nations, 174-75
religion in, 117-21
self-discipline in, 74
social and economic reform in,
56, 66-67
and Soviet Union, compared, 38,
39, 44-48
stability of, 9-10, 21, 27
surveillance of religious bodies in,
85
threat of total war and, 46
U.S. policy toward, 140, 141-42,
146, 159
China, Nationalist, 69, 74, 175
Christening, socialist, 89-90
Christian Democratic Union, East
Germany, 122-24
Christian realism, 122-25
Christianity
and acceptance of Jesus Christ,
126
and biblical conception of life, 79
in China, 117-21
Communism a "heresy" of, 101-2
and Communism as way of life,
51
Communist converts to, 113, 179
as Communist heresy, 101-2
concept of community and, 28,
35, 101, 123
criticisms of, 66, 67-68
and economic system, 54
eschatology of, 76
failure of, to accomplish reforms,
66
harmony of Communist ideals
and, 51, 56, 71, 79, 93, 94, 99-
100, 177
impact of Communism on, 78
indigenous movements within, 98
loyalty given to both Communism and, 57-58, 59, 61, 160
many strands of, 50
and personal appeals to Communists, 179-80
points of contradiction between
Communism and, 155, 159
precedent for approach of, to
Communism, 158-59
recognition of special ethnic or
national factors by, 98
responsibility of, 11-12, 124, 157

Christianity—*cont'd*
and social change, 53
in Soviet Union, 109, 110-13, 114,
121
use of ethic of, by Communism,
86-89
used to serve imperialist purposes, 68, 119
the worker priests, 62-64
Christianity and Communism (Cuninggim, ed.). 11
Christians and the State (Bennett),
quoted, 182-83
Chu Teh, 86
Church (es)
in China, 117-21
infiltration of, 85
radical leaders in, 95-96
relations of state and, 111, 116,
119-20, 121, 160-61
in U.S.S.R., 110-13
Churchill, Winston, quoted, 132
Civil liberty, danger to, in anti-
Communist activities, 24-25
see also Freedom *and* Liberty
Class collaboration, 38-39
Class-consciousness, 63, 102
Class struggle, 36, 45, 79, 80, 103-4
Clergy, Soviet, 112-13
Coexistence, 17, 18, 45, 47, 127-32,
163, 177
Cold war, 18, 48, 55, 66, 68-69, 79,
84, 128, 131, 135, 139, 146, 159,
161, 164
Collective security, 147
Collectivity
idealization of, 33
roots of, in Russian history, 116
Colonialism, 52-55, 119, 135-37
Communes, 44, 47
Communism
accommodation to, 125-26
and "American capitalism," 55
anti-colonial emphasis of, 52-55
and authoritarianism, 75-76
and Catholic Church, 57-58, 59,
61, 87, 114-15, 160
changes to come in, 182-83
in China. *See* China, Communist
and Christian ethics, 86-89, 179-
80
as Christian heresy, 101-2
compatibility of religion and, 57-
59, 114-15, 119, 120, 121, 122,
160

Communism—*cont'd*
  and concentration of power, 149, 153
  and concept of community, 28, 33, 34-35, 64, 66
  conflicting judgments of, 72-73, 86-89
  contradiction of Christianity and, 155, 159
  conversions to Christianity from, 113, 179
  differing views of, according to legal status, 23-26, 54, 61, 81
  dynamism of, 9, 27, 29, 40, 81
  efforts to define, 50-51
  faith in mission of, 35
  feeling of inevitability of, 59, 65
  and fellow travelers, 93-97
  "front" organizations of, 91-92
  goal of, 99-100
  and historical materialism, 36-39
  hostility of, to religion, 11, 12, 67-68, 105-6, 107, 113, 159
  idealism of, 56-57, 69-70
  ideology of, 38, 43, 48-50, 104-5
  impact of, on Christianity, 78
  infiltration by, 84-86
  intellectual appeal of, 73
  international, 10-11, 16, 23, 39, 40, 41, 42, 80
  legal status of, 20, 23-26, 81
  many forms of, 43-44
  mixed values in, 78-79
  moral appeal of, 73-74
  and nationalism, 37, 39-42
  nonmonolithic character of, 41-44, 116
  not wholly a slave ideology, 151
  and Orthodox Church, 75, 99, 111, 112, 113
  propaganda used by, 81-84
  pure, 47, 48, 51
  as a religion, 56
  ritual used by, 89-91
  Russian, historical perspective of, 28, 29, 30-34, 35, 116
  Russian and Chinese, compared, 38, 39, 44-48
  satellite countries under, 137
  self-sacrifice and, 64-65, 70
  shared goals of Christianity and, 51, 56, 71, 79, 93, 94, 99-100, 177
  and social reform, 66-67, 71, 74, 76
  and Soviet achievement, 56
  "stomach," 63-64
  strength of, 18-23

Communism—*cont'd*
  support of, in Italy and France, 59-62, 65, 70-71
  teaching of, in U.S., 177-78
  in U.S., 22, 23-26, 54, 81
  in villages, 33
  and worker priests, 62-64
  workers' opinions on, 70-71
  in Yugoslavia, 43, 44
  see also Soviet Union
Communism and the Churches (Roy), 85
Communist party
  in Africa and Asia, 20-21
  as an economic party, 71
  in Europe, 19-20
  in Latin America, 21-22, 25
  in U.S., 114-16
  in U.S.S.R., 15-17, 37, 108, 110
Communist Youth Federation, Argentina, 25
Community
  Christian concept of, 28, 35, 101, 123
  Communist concept of, 28, 33, 34-35, 64, 66
  in Muslim society, 116, 117
Competition, economic, 17, 129, 130, 131, 161-63
Compromise, moral, 84, 94, 103-4, 125-26
Conditioning
  education as, 176
  of religion by culture, 94
Confucianism, 118
Congo, 43
Conquest of territory, 136
Conservatism, 152
Conspiracy, 28, 37, 91
Constitutionalism, 144
Conversions
  between Christianity and Communism, 113, 179
  Christian zeal for, 157
Costa Rica, 144
Counts, George S., quoted, 35
Crime, U.S., 181
Cuba, 14, 18, 22, 136, 137
Cultural change, 125-26, 152
Cultural interchange, 166-67
Culture
  accommodation to, 125-26
  regeneration of, 100, 101, 130, 176

Daily Worker, quoted, 85

Defense, national, 169-71
Delinquency, U.S., 181
Democracy
continuing efforts to build, 181-82
and economic system, 54
education aimed at cultivating, 176
and individualism, 55
Lenin and, 38
social, 100, 102
as a venture in faith, 167
Democratic centralism, 38
Democratic socialism, 21, 51, 102, 178
Denmark, 19
Determinism, economic, 105
Deterrence, 14, 129
Dialectic materialism, 99, 101, 104-5, 124
Dictatorship, 33-34, 35, 36, 37, 176
Diplomacy
defined, 133
as instrument in cold war, 18
"quiet," 171-72
see also United States, foreign policy of
Diplomatic recognition, 140-46
as instrument of national policy, 142, 146
right to, 143, 144
Disarmament, 75, 84, 170
Djilas, 153
Dostoevski, 34
Douglas, Paul H., 175
Dulles, John Foster, 159

East Germany, 90, 122-25
Economic competition, 17, 129, 130, 131, 161-63
Economic determinism, 105
Economic World, quoted, 169
Education
antireligious, 105-6, 107, 113
in Communism, 177-78
in Soviet Union, 16, 40, 48, 105-6, 107, 113, 176
in U.S., 176, 177-78
Eisenhower, Dwight D., 165
Ends and means, 77, 83, 103, 134, 148-49
Engels, Friedrich, 110
Eschatology
Christian, 76
Communist, 33, 99
Espionage, 84, 103, 161

Ethics
Christian and Communist, 86-89, 115, 179-80
and national policy, 138
Europe
Communism in, 19-20, 27
Eastern, American trade with, 163
Evangelism, 88
Existentialism, 38
Exploitation
colonial, 137
Communist exposure of, 25-26
of French workers, 70

Far East, 21
see also China
Fascism, 11
Federal Bureau of Investigation, 23, 85
Fellow travelers, 93-97
Feuerbach, 102
Foreign aid, 26, 167-69
France
Communism in, 19, 63-64, 65, 70-71
worker priests in, 62-64
Frankel, Max, quoted, 66
Free enterprise, 163
Free trade, 163
"Free World," 150, 151
Freedom
and American way of life, 55
and anti-Communist activities, 24-25
of antireligious propaganda, 121
of individual "witness," 95
of religion, 107, 110, 115, 119, 120, 121
and renunciation of individual liberty, 134
"Front" organizations, 91-92
Fukien Province, 88, 89

Great Britain
Chinese hostility to, 68
Communism in, 19
Gresham's law, 149
Group leadership, 116
Guatemala, 87

Hackworth, G. H., quoted, 143-44
Hegel, 101, 110
Henry, Patrick, 128
Heresy
Christian or Communist, 101-2
theological, 105

Higgins, George G., quoted, 177-78
Historical materialism, 36-39, 99, 101
History, "devil theory of," 159
Hocking, William Ernest, 157
Hook, Sidney, 128
Hromádka, Joseph L., quoted, 100
Hudson, G. F., quoted, 46, 47
Hughes, Charles Evans, quoted, 144-45
Hull, Cordell, quoted, 144
Human Rights, Declaration of, 136
Humphrey, Hubert, 47, 131
Hungarian revolt, 20, 53, 76
Huss, 105
Hyde, Charles Cheney, quoted, 143, 145-46

Idealism
  Communist, 56-57, 69-70
  democratic, 181-82
Ideology
  cold war and, 66
  Communist and Western, 104-5, 129
  role of, 43, 48-50
Imperialism
  Russian, 43
  United States, 36
  Western, and Christianity, 68, 119
Incentive, 47
Income, discrepancies in, 65
India
  Communist party in, 20-21, 39
  socialism in, 21, 178
"Indirect aggression," 139-40
Individual freedom of witness, 95
Individualism, 34-35
  of the church, 107
  and democracy, 55
  and responsibility, 134
Indoctrination, Communist, 49
Indonesia, 21, 85
Industrialization, 124
Infiltration, 84-86, 96
Insecurity, 55, 76
Intellectuals
  appeal of Communism to, 55, 73
  as fellow travelers, 93
  leadership of, 37
Inter-American Peace Committee, 26
Interdependence of nations, 132
International character of Communism, 10-11, 16, 23, 39, 40, 41, 42, 80

International exchange plans, 166-67
International relations, 134-35, 169
  and diplomatic recognition, 140-46
  and nationalism, 41
International sanctions, 132
Iraq, 20, 89
Ireland, 19
Irresponsibility
  national and individual, 134
  neutralism as, 147
Islam, 116-17
Islam in Modern History (Smith), quoted, 116, 117
Italy, 19, 45, 59-62, 65, 160

Jefferson, Thomas, 142, 143, 144, 146, 153, 160
Jesus, 107, 108, 123, 126
Jews in Soviet Union, 99
Judaism, 51, 99

Kautsky, 102
Kerala, 21, 24
Khrushchev, Nikita, 39, 48, 50, 161
  on coexistence, 130, 131
  on communes, 47
  on incentive, 47
  proposals of, for trade agreement, 165, 166
  at United Nations, 75, 82
Kingsley, Charles, 106
Kohn, Hans, quoted, 15, 32, 33, 34
Koinonia, 35
Korean War, 83

Labor unions, 19, 60, 72
Land reform, 60
Lapland, 20
Latin America
  Communism in, 21-22, 26, 87
  and Monroe Doctrine, 137-40
  political restiveness in, 172-73
  U.S. recognition of governments in, 144
League of Militant Godless, 11
League of Nations, 133
Lenin, 37-38, 176
Leo XIII, 87
Liberty
  civil, 24-25
  differing views of, 67
  religious, 107, 110, 115, 119, 120, 121
  renunciation of, and freedom, 134

Lincoln, Abraham, 181
Linton, Ralph, quoted, 155-56, 157
Lippmann, Walter, 43, 126, 128, 139, 172
Lowrie, Donald A., quoted, 114
Loyalty oath to East German government, 125
Lutheran churches, 121

McKinley, William, 132
Manifest destiny, 36
  see also Imperialism
Mao Tse-tung, 23, 39, 46, 119
Maremma, 69
Maritain, Jacques, 101
Marshall, George C., quoted, 168
Marshall Plan, 168
Marx, Karl, 39, 40, 43, 45, 68, 101, 107, 123, 124
Marxism (-Leninism) , 28, 33, 40, 43, 50, 73, 79, 102, 106, 113, 118, 124
Masaryk, Thomas, quoted, 32-33
Materialism, 33, 36-39, 99, 101, 104-5, 113, 124
Means and ends, 77, 83, 103, 134, 148-49
Meissen declaration, 122-25
Messianism, Russian, 33, 34, 35, 40, 155
Michael, Archangel, 108
Middle ages, monasteries in, 105
Middle class, support of Communism by, 59-60
Millis, Walter, quoted, 169-70
Missionary movement, 35
  Christian, 53, 68, 98, 118, 119, 157, 179
  Communist, 56, 87, 88-89
  and imperialism, 68, 119
Monasteries, 105
Monroe Doctrine, 137-40
Moral appeal of Communism, 73-74
Moral Man and Immoral Society (Niebuhr) , 133
Morality
  evolutionary concept of, 104
  obligation of U.S. to approach, 181-82
  shared, of Christianity and Communism, 115
  Western, vulnerability of, 77, 93-94
Morrison, Robert, 119
Moscow as "Third Rome," 34
Murdock, George P., quoted, 156
Murray, John Courtney, quoted, 80

Muslims, 116-17

Name-giving dedication, 90
Napoleon, 38
Nasser, Gamal Abdel, 73
National Catholic Welfare Conference, 177
National defense, 169-71
National interest, 132-35, 142, 148, 166, 168-69, 172
Nationalism, 34, 37, 39-42, 48, 68, 132-34, 178
Nationalist China, 69, 74, 175
Naturalism, 104-5
Nazism, 11, 83
Near East, 20
Nechaev, 30
Negroes, the Scottsboro case, 92
Nehru, Jawaharlal, 53, 73
Nestorianism, 119
Netherlands, 19
Neutralism, 21, 146-48
New Class (Djilas) , 153
Nicolai, Metropolitan, 111
Niebuhr, Reinhold, 133
Nihilism, 30-32, 33
Nixon, Richard, 163
Nomad, Max, 44, 149, 152-53
Nonalignment, 21
Nonrecognition
  of Communist China, 146
  of Soviet Union, 145
North Korea, 21, 27
North Vietnam, 21
Norway, 20
Nuclear deterrence, 14, 129
Nuclear stalemate, 14, 79
Nuclear testing, 170, 174

Organization of American States, 26, 138, 139
Orthodox Church, 34, 75, 99, 110-11, 112, 113
Other worldliness, opposition to, 105-6, 108
Oxford Conference essentials of religious liberty, 120

Pares, Bernard, quoted, 33
Paul, 99, 108, 151
Peiping (Peking) , 85, 86
Personalism, 34-35
Personality
  cult of, 48
  transformation of, 76, 99, 176
Philippine Islands, 36, 136

Philosophy, Communist and Western, 104-5, 129
Pierce, Franklin, quoted, 143
Poland
American trade with, 163
Communism in, 41
Political maturity, 133, 135
Politics, low opinion of, 133
Politics of Despair (Cantril), 57
Polyani, Michael, quoted, 76-77
Population
in China, 46-47
explosion in, 52
Poverty, 55, 59-61, 169
Power
corrupting effect of, 149, 152, 153
limiting of, 134
Pravda, 16, 23, 82-83
Prestige, 156, 181
Proletariat
dictatorship of, 37, 176
international, 40, 80
Propaganda
anti-Communist, 96
antireligious, 111, 121
as an aspect of diplomacy, 172
Communist, 25, 81-84, 86-87, 128-29, 176
missionary, 68
as public relations between nations, 83
Property rights, 103
Protestantism, 35, 99, 123-24
in China, 117-19
in U.S.S.R., 111, 112, 113

Race relations, U.S., 55, 181
Racketeering, U.S., 181
Rauschenbusch, 66
Realism
Christian, 122-25
facing facts, 151-52
in revolution, 153-54
Recognition of governments. See Diplomatic recognition
Reform
land, 60
social, 66-67, 71, 74, 76, 93, 99, 123
Reissig, Herman F., quoted, 73
Rejection, feeling of, 65
Religion
arts and, 108-9
attempts to define, 57-58
Communist antagonism to, 11, 12, 67-68, 105-6, 107, 113, 159

Religion—*cont'd*
conditioned by culture, 94
faith in mission of, 35
freedom of individual "witness" in, 95
not incompatible with Communist membership, 51, 56, 57-59, 71, 79, 93, 94, 99-100, 160, 177
progressive role of, 105
reduced opposition to, 110, 111
separated from all other areas, 114
Soviet policy on, 107-14
vitality of, in U.S.S.R., 114
see also Catholic Church, Christianity, Church (es), Judaism, Orthodox Church, *and* Protestantism
Religious liberty, essentials of, 120
Responsibility
Christian, 11-12, 124, 157
in education, 177-78
moral, in building democracy, 181-82
Revisionism, 43
Revolution
ambivalence of U.S. attitude toward, 152
both good and bad in, 154-55
Chinese, background of, 67-69
evil in, 149, 152-53
of expectation, 52
realism in, 153-54
Russian, 29
and social change, 54
world, 39, 40
Ricci, Matthew, 119
Rio de Janeiro, Treaty of, 138
Ritual, Communist, 89-91
Roosevelt, Franklin D., 145
Rousseau, 38
Roy, Ralph Lord, 85, 92
Royce, Josiah, 28
Russell, Bertrand, 128
Russian Revolution, 29

Satellite territories, 137
Scotland, 72
Scottsboro case, 92
Schlesinger, Arthur, Jr., quoted, 41-42
Science and technology, 52, 56
Secularism, 58
Self-criticism, U.S., 181
Self-discipline, 74
Self-government, readiness for, 137

Self-sacrifice, 64-65, 70, 74, 88, 118
Sergius, Metropolitan, 110
Shanghai, 69
Sino-Indian border dispute, 21
Smith, W. Cantwell, quoted, 116, 117
Smith Act, 23-24
Sobornost, 33
Social Democrats, Russia, 38
Social-gospel movement, 10ⁿ
Social injustice, 70, 92, 137
Social reform, 66-67, 71, 74, 76, 93, 99, 123
Social stability and instability, 54
Socialism
  democratic, 21, 51, 102, 178
  distinction between Communism and, 48, 51
  economic competition with, 17, 129, 130, 131, 161-63
  in India, 21, 178
  "in one country," 40
  and regeneration of society, 130
  struggle of, with capitalism, 45
Socialist christening, 89-90
Socialist Unity Party, East Germany, 90
Society, regeneration of, 100, 101, 130, 176
Solidarity, working-class, 61, 62, 63, 64
South Africa, 20
South China, 88
Sovereignty, 133-34, 135
Soviet Union
  American image of, 56, 73
  attitude of, toward religion, 99, 107-14
  churches in, 110-13
  Communist doctrine in, 15-17
  compared with China, 38, 39, 44-48
  conflict of, with China, 40, 41
  Constitution of, 121
  cultural and political separation of, from West, 15, 55
  education in, 16, 40, 48, 105-6, 107, 113, 176
  emphasis of, on abolition of colonialism, 53
  foreign policy of, 28
  historical background of Communism in, 28, 29, 30-34, 35
  image of, in underdeveloped countries, 72-73
  interpretation of coexistence by,

Soviet Union—*cont'd*
  129, 130
  Muslims in, 116-17
  nationalism in, 48
  the new Soviet man, 66, 99
  Orthodox Church in, 34, 75, 99, 110-11, 113
  power of, and Communist ideology, 43
  relation of U.S. and, 159
  rise of an elite in, 36-37
  stability of regime in, 9, 27, 42-43
  successes of, 56
  threat of total war and, 46
  trade with, 163-66
  and United Nations, 173-74
  U.S. recognition of, 145-46
  see also Communism
Spanish-American War, 136
Stalin, 43, 47, 48, 73, 110, 111
State Department, U.S., 139, 141, 142, 145
Stereotypes of Soviet Union and China, 56
Stevenson, Adlai, 26, 173n., 175
Strong, Josiah, 36
Student Christian Association, 88
Student-exchange programs, 166-67
Sulzberger, C. L., 45
"Summitry," 171
Supernatural emphasis. *See* Other worldliness
Supreme Court
  school-segregation cases, 136
  Smith Act decision, 23
Survey, Morgan Guaranty Trust Company, quoted, 44
Sweden, 20

T'ai Tsung, 119
Taiwan, 175
Tang dynasty, 119
Temple, William, 101
"Thematic" values, 155-56
Theological schools, U.S.S.R., 112
Three-Self-Movement, 120
Tibet, 21
Times (New York), 146, 147
Titoism, 43, 44, 50
Togliatti, 45
Totalitarianism, 10-11, 28, 33-34, 37, 42-48, 118, 176
Trade, East-West, 163-66, 167
Trade unions, 19, 60, 72
Trusteeship territories, 136
Truth, two kinds of, 76-77

Underdeveloped countries, aid to, 167-69
"United front," 91
United Nations, 132, 133, 135, 137, 147
  and Korean War, 83
  new nations in, 173
  problem of admitting Communist China to, 174-75
  and Soviet Union, 173-74
  and U.S., 172-75
United States
  acquisition of Cuba and Philippines by, 136
  aid programs of, 167-69
  ambivalent attitude of, to revolution, 152
  capitalism in, 55
  Communist Party in, 114-16
  Constitution of, 160-61
  and cultural interchange, 166-67
  diplomacy in, 18, 171-72
  diplomatic recognition by, 140-46
  educational responsibility of, 176, 177-78
  evaluation of policies of, 127-49
  foreign policy of, 59, 132-35, 137-46, 147
  "front" organizations in, 91-92
  guilt in, over use of atomic bomb, 103
  history of, and Communism, 29
  image of Soviet Union in, 56, 73
  imperialism of, 35-36
  and Latin America, 26, 137-40, 144
  Monroe Doctrine, 137-40
  moral obligations of, 181-82
  national defense, 169-71
  national interest and sovereignty of, 132-35, 142, 166
  neutrality of, 147
  "quiet diplomacy" of, 171-72
  race problem in, 55, 181
  relation of Soviet Union and, 159
  status of Communism in, 22, 23-26, 54, 81
  support of dictatorships by, 59
  trade of, with Eastern Europe, 163-66, 167
  and United Nations, 172-75
Unity
  of human race, 155
  working-class, 61, 62, 63, 64

Values
  mixed, in Communism, 78-79
  universal, 155-57
  Western, 67
Venezuela, 21

Wadsworth, James J., quoted, 173n., 174
Wall Street Journal, quoted, 43-44
Wan Li, 119
War
  danger of, 170
  difference between peace and, 79
  futility of, 159
  ideology and, 129
  just and unjust, 45, 159
  rejection of inevitability of, 17, 44-46, 75, 129, 131
  substitution of economic competition for, 161-63
  as suicide, 82
  suspension of ethics in, 103
  total, 149
  two levels of, 79
Welfare state, 46
Wells, H. G., 177
West
  need of, to face realities, 151-52
  philosophy in, 104
  question of truth-telling in, 77, 93-94
Wilson, Woodrow, 143, 144, 171
Witness (Chambers), quoted, 69-70
Wolfe, Bertram D., 37, 38
Work, value of, 63
Worker priests, 62-64
Working-class solidarity, 61, 62, 63, 64
World Council for the Defense of Peace, 111
World revolution, 39, 40
World War II, 40, 91, 110
World Without War (Millis), quoted, 169-70
Wright, Arthur, quoted, 42
Wright, Quincy, 146, 147-48

Yardstick, quoted, 177-78
Yenching Campus, 88
Young Communist League, 85
Youth dedication, East Germany, 90
Yugoslavia, 41, 43, 44